KS3 Maths is Easy

(Ratio, Proportion & Rates of Change)

www.How2Become.com

As part of this product you have also received FREE access to online tests that will help you to pass Key Stage 3 MATHS *(Ratio, Proportion & Rates of Change).*

To gain access, simply go to:

www.MyEducationalTests.co.uk

Get more products for passing any test at:

www.How2Become.com

Orders: Please contact How2Become Ltd, Suite 14, 50 Churchill Square Business Centre, Kings Hill, Kent ME19 4YU.

You can order through Amazon.co.uk under ISBN: 9781911259244, via the website www.How2Become.com or through Gardners.com.

ISBN: 9781911259244

First published in 2017 by How2Become Ltd.

Copyright © 2017 How2Become.

All rights reserved. Apart from any permitted use under UK copyright law, no part of this publication may be reproduced or transmitted in any form or by any means, electronic or mechanical, including photocopying, recording, or any information, storage or retrieval system, without permission in writing from the publisher or under licence from the Copyright Licensing Agency Limited. Further details of such licenses (for reprographic reproduction) may be obtained from the Copyright Licensing Agency Ltd, Saffron House, 6-10 Kirby Street, London EC1N 8TS.

Typeset by How2Become Ltd.
Printed and bound by CPI Group (UK) Ltd, Croydon, CR0 4YY

Disclaimer

Every effort has been made to ensure that the information contained within this guide is accurate at the time of publication. How2Become Ltd is not responsible for anyone failing any part of any selection process as a result of the information contained within this guide. How2Become Ltd and their authors cannot accept any responsibility for any errors or omissions within this guide, however caused. No responsibility for loss or damage occasioned by any person acting, or refraining from action, as a result of the material in this publication can be accepted by How2Become Ltd.

The information within this guide does not represent the views of any third party service or organisation.

Contains public sector information licensed under the Open Government Licence v3.0.

CONTENTS

Understanding The Curriculum	7
Increase your Chances	19
Learn your Maths Terminology	25
Ratios	29
• *Understanding Ratios*	30
• *Ratio of Shapes*	37
• *Simplifying Ratios*	45
• *Ratios and Scaling*	53
• *Proportional Division*	59
Proportion	65
• *Direct Proportion*	66
• *Indirect (Inverse) Proportion*	71
Percentage Change	77
• *Percentage Increase*	78
• *Percentage Decrease*	89
• *Adding Interest*	99
• *Change in Value*	105
Metric and Imperial Units	117
Speed, Distance and Time	129
Density, Mass and Volume	139
Maps and Scaling	149

UNDERSTANDING THE CURRICULUM

THE NATIONAL CURRICULUM

State-funded schools are governed by a set curriculum of 'core' subjects which form part of a child's education. These core subjects are essential for providing key knowledge and skills, which in turn will help us to produce well-rounded and educated citizens.

In Key Stage 3 (ages 11-14), the core subjects that must be taught in schools include the following:

- **English**
- **Maths**
- **Science**
- **Art and Design**
- **Citizenship**
- **Computing**
- **Design and Technology**
- **Languages**
- **Geography**
- **History**
- **Music**
- **Physical Education**

All schools, from Key Stage 1 to Key Stage 4, must also teach Religious Studies to their students. From the age of 11, children will also be taught Sex Education. However, parents are given the option of pulling their children out from Religious Studies and Sex Education.

THE IMPORTANCE OF MATHS

Maths is an integral subject within the national curriculum. Students should be able to understand the key concepts and different mathematical formula, in order to enhance their knowledge and increase their cognitive ability.

By achieving a strong level of understanding, students are able to convey their mathematical knowledge in a range of other subjects

UNDERSTANDING THE CURRICULUM

including science, computing, and geography.

The fundamental aims of the Maths subject include:

- Using arithmetic to solve problems;
- Understanding the difference between accuracy and estimation;
- Expressing arithmetic using algebraic equations and formula;
- Learning how to carefully lay out sets of data using graphs and charts;
- Understanding averages in terms of mean, mode, median and range;
- Improving children's basic mathematical skills, before advancing on to more technical and challenging mathematical concepts;
- Improving children's confidence in their mathematical abilities, allowing them to grasp different topics of maths and how they can apply these techniques to their work.

In Key Stage 3, maths is broken down into several modules:

- **Numbers and Calculations;**
- **Ratio, Proportion and Rates of Change;**
- **Geometry and Measures;**
- **Working with Algebra;**
- **Probability and Statistics.**

The aforementioned modules are all used to teach students the vital skills for both academia and the outside world.

Pupils will be able to recognise different mathematic concepts and apply them to different calculations. In Key Stage 3, it is important that students are able to move fluently through the subject, and demonstrate a wide range of skills.

Key Stage 3 is a crucial time in academic terms, as it prepares students for their GCSEs. Every pupil will be required to take Maths as a GCSE, and therefore having a strong knowledge in these starter years at secondary school, will put students in the position that they are expected to be in before entering their GCSEs.

MATHS SUBJECT CONTENT

Below we have broken down the aims and objectives of each 'module' for Maths. This will hopefully give you some idea of what will be assessed, and how you can improve different areas in the mathematics subject.

PROBABILITY AND STATISTICS

Pupils will be taught how to:

☐ Understand the probability of an outcome.

☐ Record, describe and analyse the frequency of outcomes of simple probability experiments involving randomness, fairness, equally and unequally outcomes, using mathematical language, and the use of a probability scale from 0-1.

☐ Enumerate data and understand information provided in the form of:

- *Tables, grids, graphs and charts, Venn diagrams and pictograms.*

☐ Describe, interpret and compare information from graphical representations.

☐ Understand the mean, mode, median and range of a set of data, and comparing this to other similar data.

☐ Construct graphs and charts in order to represent a set of data. Pupils should understand what type of graph or chart works best for the data they have collated.

UNDERSTANDING THE CURRICULUM

NUMBERS AND CALCULATIONS

Pupils will be taught how to:

☐ Apply the concepts of the following mathematical numbers:

- *Prime numbers, factors, multiples, common factors, common multiples, highest common factor (HCF), lowest common multiple (LCM) and prime factorisation.*

☐ Use place values for working out decimals, measures and integers of any size.

☐ Order numbers in terms of positive and negative. Students should also have a strong grasp of mathematical symbols including:

=, ≠, ≤, ≥

☐ Use brackets, powers, roots and reciprocals.

☐ Use different standard units of measure including:

- *Mass, length, time and money.*

☐ Round numbers up and down to the correct degree of accuracy. Students will be taught about significant figures and decimal places.

☐ Correctly use a calculator, and learn all of the key buttons on a scientific calculator.

☐ Interpret percentages as being 'a number out of 100'. Pupils will also be taught how to use percentages higher than 100%, how to convert a percentage into a fraction or decimal, and how to find the percentage of a number.

☐ Recognise square and cube numbers, and understanding the importance of powers 2, 3, 4 and 5.

☐ Appreciate the infinite nature of the sets of integers, real and rational numbers.

☐ Interpret and compare numbers in standard form $A \times 10^N$ $1 \leq A < 10$, where N is a positive or negative integer or zero.

RATIO, PROPORTION AND RATES OF CHANGE

Pupils will be taught how to:

☐ Change between different standard units. For example:

- *Length, area, time volume and mass.*

☐ Use ratio notation, including reduction to simplest form.

☐ Use scale factors, scale diagrams and maps.

☐ Express one quantity as a fraction of another, where the fraction is less than 1 and greater than 1.

☐ Divide a given quantity into two parts in given part:part or part:whole ratio; express the division of a quantity into two parts as a ratio.

☐ Understand that a multiplicative relationship between two quantities can be expressed as a ratio or a fraction.

☐ Relate the language of ratios and the associated calculations to the arithmetic of fractions and to linear functions.

☐ Solve problems involving percentage change including:

- *Percentage increase, percentage decrease, original value problems and simple interest in financial mathematics.*

☐ Solve problems involving direct and inverse proportion, including graphical and algebraic representations.

☐ Using compound units such as speed, unit pricing and density to solve problems.

WORKING WITH ALGEBRA

Pupils will be taught how to:

☐ Use and interpret algebraic notations, including:

- *ab in place of a x b;*
- *3y in place of y + y + y and 3 x y;*
- *a^2 in place of a x a, a3 in place of a x a x a, a^2b in place of a x a x b;*
- *a/b in place of a ÷ b;*
- *Coefficients written as fractions rather than as decimals;*
- *Brackets.*

☐ Substitute numerical values into formulae and expressions, including scientific formulae.

☐ Understand and use the concepts and vocabulary of expressions, equations, inequalities, terms and factors.

☐ Simplify and manipulate algebraic expressions to maintain equivalence by:

- *Collecting like terms;*
- *Multiplying a single term over a bracket;*
- *Taking out common factors;*
- *Expanding products of two or more binomials.*

☐ Recognise, sketch and produce graphs of linear and quadratic functions of one variable with appropriate scaling, using equations in x and y and the Cartesian plane.

☐ Use linear and quadratic graphs to estimate values of y for given values of x and vice versa and to find approximate solutions of simultaneous linear equations.

☐ Recognise arithmetic sequences and find the nth term.

☐ Find approximate solutions to contextual problems from given graphs of a variety of functions, including piece-wise linear, exponential and reciprocal graphs.

☐ Reduce a given linear equation in two variables to the standard form y = mx + c; calculate and interpret gradients and intercepts of graphs of such linear equations numerically, graphically and algebraically.

☐ Recognise geometric sequences and appreciate other sequences that arise.

GEOMETRY AND MEASURES

Pupils will be taught how to:

☐ Derive and apply formulae to calculate and solve problems involving;

- *Perimeter and area of triangles, parallelograms, trapezia, volume of cuboids (including cubes) and other prisms (including cylinders).*

☐ Calculate and solve problems involving: perimeters of 2D shapes (including circles), areas of circles and composite shapes.

☐ Draw and measure line segments and angles in geometric figures, including interpreting scale drawings.

☐ Derive and use the standard ruler and compass constructions (perpendicular bisector of a line segment, constructing a perpendicular to a given line from/at a given point, bisecting a given angle); recognise and use the perpendicular distance from a point to a line as the shortest distance to the line.

☐ Describe, sketch and draw using conventional terms and notations:

- *Points, lines, parallel lines, perpendicular lines, right angles, regular polygons, and other polygons that are reflectively and rotationally symmetric.*

☐ Use the standard convention for labelling the sides and angles of triangle ABC, and know and use the criteria for congruence of triangles.

☐ Derive and illustrate properties of triangles, quadrilaterals, circles and other place figures [for example, equal lengths and angles] using appropriate language and technologies.

☐ Use Pythagoras' Theorem and trigonometric ratios in similar triangles to solve problems involving right-angled triangles.

☐ Use properties of faces, surfaces, edges and vertices of cubes, cuboids, prisms, cylinders, pyramids, cones and spheres to solve problems in 3D.

☐ Interpret mathematical relationships both algebraically and geometrically.

☐ Identify properties of, and describe the results of, translations, rotations and reflections applied to given figures.

☐ Identify and construct triangles, and construct congruent triangles, and construct similar shapes by enlargements, with and without coordinate grids.

☐ Apply the properties of angles at a point, angles at a point on a straight line, vertically opposite angles.

☐ Understand and use the relationship between parallel lines and alternate and corresponding angles.

Maths is not only a core subject in schools, but is also a topic that impacts upon every aspect of our daily lives. As you can see, it is imperative that students are able to engage in mathematics, in order to improve on vital skills and knowledge.

USING THIS GUIDE

This guide focuses specifically on Key Stage 3 Maths (Ratio, Proportion & Rates of Change). This book will cover everything you need to know in terms of Ratios, Proportions and Rates of Change.

REMEMBER – It's important that you have a good mathematical understanding, as this will help you through other school subjects, and in day-to-day activities.

HOW WILL I BE ASSESSED?

At Key Stage 3, children will be assessed based on Levels. These years do not count towards anything, and are simply a reflection of progression and development. The first years of secondary school are in place in order to determine whether or not pupils are meeting the minimum requirements, and are therefore an integral stage for preparing pupils for their GCSE courses.

Although these years do not count towards any final results, they do go a long way in deciphering which GCSEs you will pick up. For example, if you were excelling in Maths at KS3, you could consider taking this subject at A Level, and even Higher Education!

The subjects that you choose at GCSE will impact upon your future aspirations, including further education and career opportunities.

UNDERSTANDING THE CURRICULUM

You will be monitored and assessed throughout these schooling years, via the following:

- Ongoing teacher assessments;
- Term progress reports;
- Summative assessments at the end of each academic year.

By the end of Key Stage 3, pupils are expected to achieve Levels 5 or 6.

INCREASE YOUR CHANCES

KS3 Maths Is Easy (Ratio, Proportion & Rates of Change)

Below is a list of GOLDEN NUGGETS that will help YOU and your CHILD to prepare for Key Stage 3 Maths.

Golden Nugget 1 – Revision timetables

When it comes to revising, preparation is key. That is why you need to sit down with your child and come up with an efficient and well-structured revision timetable.

It is important that you work with your child to assess their academic strengths and weaknesses, in order to carry out these revision sessions successfully.

> *TIP – Focus on their weaker areas first!*
>
> *TIP – Create a weekly revision timetable to work through different subject areas.*
>
> *TIP – Spend time revising with your child. Your child will benefit from your help and this is a great way for you to monitor their progress.*

Golden Nugget 2 – Understanding the best way your child learns

There are many different ways to revise when it comes to exams, and it all comes down to picking a way that your child will find most useful.

Below is a list of the common learning styles that you may want to try with your child:

- **Visual** – the use of pictures and images to remember information.
- **Aural** – the use of sound and music to remember information.
- **Verbal** – the use of words, in both speech and writing, to understand information.
- **Social** – working together in groups.
- **Solitary** – working and studying alone.

Popular revision techniques include: *mind mapping, flash cards, making notes, drawing flow charts,* and *diagrams*. You could instruct your child on how to turn diagrams and pictures into words, and words into diagrams. Try as many different methods as possible, to see which style your child learns from the most.

> *TIP* – Work out what kind of learner your child is. What method will they benefit from the most?
>
> *TIP* – Try a couple of different learning aids and see if you notice a change in your child's ability to understand what is being taught.

Golden Nugget 3 – Break times

Allow your child plenty of breaks when revising.

It's really important not to overwork your child.

> *TIP* – Practising for 10 to 15 minutes per day will improve your child's reading ability.
>
> *TIP* – Keep in mind that a child's retention rate is usually between 30 to 50 minutes. Any longer than this, and your child will start to lose interest.

Golden Nugget 4 – Practice, practice and more practice!

Purchase past practice papers. This is a fantastic way for you to gain an idea of how your child is likely to be tested.

Golden Nugget 5 – Understanding different areas in Maths

As with any subject, Maths has a range of different modules. Therefore, your child may find one module easier than another. We recommend that you spend time focusing on one module at a time. This will ensure that your child knows everything they should about each module – before moving on to the next.

> *TIP* – Know what modules you need to focus on!

Golden Nugget 6 – Improve their confidence

Encourage your child to interact with you, their peers and their teachers. If they are struggling, they need to be able to reach out and ask for help. By asking for help, they will be able to work on their weaknesses, and therefore increase their overall performance and confidence.

TIP – Talk to your child and work through different Maths questions with them.

Golden Nugget 7 – Stay positive!

The most important piece of preparation advice we can give you, is to make sure that your child is positive and relaxed about these tests.

Don't let assessments worry you, and certainly don't let them worry your child.

TIP – Make sure the home environment is as comfortable and relaxed as possible for your child.

Golden Nugget 8 – Answer the easier questions first

A good tip to teach your child is to answer all the questions they find easiest first. That way, they can swiftly work through the paper, before attempting the questions they struggle with.

TIP – Get your child to undergo a practice paper. Tell them to fill in the answers that they find the easiest first. That way, you can spend time helping your child with the questions they find more difficult.

Spend some time working through the questions they find difficult and make sure that they know how to work out the answer.

Golden Nugget 9 – Understanding mathematical terminology

The next section is a glossary containing all the mathematical terminology that your child should familiarise themselves with.

INCREASE YOUR CHANCES

Sit down with your child and learn as many of these KEY TERMS as you can.

TIP – Why not make your child's learning fun? Write down all of the terms and cut them out individually. Do the same for the definitions.

Get your child to try and match the KEY TERM with its definition. Keep playing this game until they get them all right!

Golden Nugget 10 – Check out our other revision resources

We have a range of other KS3 Maths resources to help your child prepare for EVERY stage of their mathematical learning.

LEARN YOUR MATHS TERMINOLOGY

ACUTE ANGLES	An angle less than 90°.
ALGEBRA	The part of maths where symbols and letters are used to represent numbers.
AREA	A measurement of a surface. For the area of a square, you would multiply the height by the width.
BIDMAS	**B**rackets, **I**ndices, **D**ivision, **M**ultiplication, **A**ddition, **S**ubtraction.
CIRCUMFERENCE	The distance around something. It is the enclosing boundary of a curved geometric figure.
COMPOUND SHAPE	A compound shape includes two or more simple shapes.
CUBED NUMBERS	A cubed number is a number multiplied by itself, three times.
DECIMAL PLACES	The position of a digit to the right of a decimal point.
DECIMAL	A type of number, for example 0.5 is equivalent to 50%.
DIAMETER	A straight line passing side-to-side through the middle of a circle.
EQUILATERAL TRIANGLE	A type of triangle. All sides and angles are of equal value. All angles are 60°.
ESTIMATION	A rough calculation or guess.
FACTOR	A factor is a number that can be divided wholly into another number. For example, 4 is a factor of 8.
FRACTIONS	A type of number, for example ½ is equivalent to a half.
FREQUENCY	The frequency of a specific data is the number of times that number occurs. (Frequent).
HIGHEST COMMON FACTOR (HCF)	To find the HCF, you need to find all of the factors of two or more numbers, and then see which number is the highest.

LEARN YOUR MATHS TERMINOLOGY

IMPERIAL UNITS	Imperial units of length, mass and capacity. Includes inch, foot, yard, ounce, pound, stone, pint and gallon.
ISOSCELES TRIANGLE	A type of triangle. Two sides and angles are of the same value.
LOWEST COMMON MULTIPLE (LCM)	To find the LCM, you need to find all of the multiples of two or more numbers, and then work out the lowest number in common.
MEAN	A type of average. Add up all of the numbers and divide it by how many numbers there are.
MEDIAN	A type of average. Rearrange the numbers in ascending order. What number is in the middle?
METRIC UNITS	Metric units of length, mass and capacity. Includes mm, cm, km, mg, g, kg, ml and litres.
MODE	A type of average. What number occurs the most?
MULTIPLE	A multiple simply means 'times tables'. The multiples of 2 are 2, 4, 6, 8 and so on.
NEGATIVE NUMBER	A negative number is a number less than 0. On a scale, positive numbers move to the right, and negative numbers move to the left. Indicated by the sign '-'. For example, -4.
OBTUSE ANGLE	A type of angle. An obtuse angle is more than 90° but less than 180°.
PARALLEL LINE	A parallel line is two or more lines that are always the same distance apart, and never touch.
PERIMETER	A measurement of a surface. The line forming the boundary of a closed geometrical figure.
PERPENDICULAR LINES	A perpendicular line is two lines that meet at a right angle (90°).
PI	The mathematic constant 3.14159... The ratio of a circle's circumference to its diameter.

POSITIVE NUMBER	A positive number is a number more than 0. On a scale, positive numbers move to the right, and negative numbers move to the left.
PROBABILITY	The extent to whether something is likely to occur.
RADIUS	The radius is a straight line.
RANGE	A type of average. The range between the largest number and the smallest number.
RATIO	The quantitative relation between two amounts showing the number of times one value contain or is contained within the other.
REFLEX ANGLE	A type of angle. A reflex angle is more than 180° but less than 360°.
RIGHT-ANGLED TRIANGLE	A type of triangle. A triangle that has a 90° angle.
SCALENE TRIANGLE	A triangle with no equal angles or equal length sides.
SIGNIFICANT FIGURES	The digits carrying meaning. This allows us get a rough idea. For example, 48,739. The '4' is a significant figure because it represents 40 thousand.
SIMPLIFYING FRACTIONS	A way of making a fraction easier to read by finding a whole number that can be divided equally into both the denominator and numerator. For example, 12/24 can be simplified to 1/2. Both '12' and '24' can be divided by 12.
SQUARED NUMBER	A square number is the number that is reached when multiplying two of the same numbers together. For example 9 is the square number of 3 x 3.
SYMMETRY	Symmetry is when one shape becomes exactly like another if it's flipped or rotated.
VOLUME	The amount of space that a shape or object occupies. Contained within a container.

UNDERSTANDING RATIOS
(RATIOS)

UNDERSTANDING RATIOS

Ratios are a way of comparing amounts of something. Ratios compare one part to another part, or compare one part in relation to something whole.

Let's go through some of the properties of some regular polygon shapes.

As you can see, we have 8 squares.

There are 4 white squares, and 4 black squares.

If we wanted to write this as a ratio we could write it as follows:

4 : 4

If you had a question asking what ratio of black squares there are to white squares, you would need to write the number of black squares first.

The key thing to remember when writing ratios, is the use of the colon.

EXAMPLE

7 : 4

The colon basically means 'to every'.

For example, Sandra has 7 sweets to Joey's 4 sweets.

UNDERSTANDING RATIOS

When it comes to ratios, there are a few things that you need to know:

- Ratios of Shapes
- Simplifying Ratios
- Scaling Up Ratios
- Proportional Division

These topics will be discussed in the next few chapters!

ACTIVITY TIME!

Below are sentences, each of which contain two amounts. Write the ratio, using the colon, as mentioned previously.

a) Tommy has 8 sweets. Polly has 3 sweets.

[   ]

b) Alesha works 42 hours a week. Her brother Jamie only works 12 hours.

[   ]

c) You need 4 parts flour to 1 part sugar.

[   ]

Question Time!

QUESTION 1

For the following sentence, write the correct ratio:

Ollie has 12 marbles. His friend Dave has only 8 marbles.

☐ : ☐

QUESTION 2

For the following sentence, write the correct ratio:

A math class hass 11 girls and 14 boys.

☐ : ☐

QUESTION 3

For the following sentence, write the correct ratio:

Peter has 6 sweets. Mikey has double.

☐ : ☐

QUESTION 4

For the following ratio, come up with a possible context:

2 : 3

UNDERSTANDING RATIOS

QUESTION 5

For the following ratio, come up with a possible context:

5 : 7

QUESTION 6

Complete the wordsearch to find all of the key words for ratios.

```
T R N L C M K F D M C C Y S F C F V I A
C W O Q N Q H Q K Y H Z R D F Q E U U C
S I S S C A L I N G A A E Z M Y X D V R
S D B L A P Q I M R V S D P P N M M O T
I K L E V S H T D R B R U J N M R C N I
S E P Y Q I S N T U N E C G T L S K R F
J U N D S I M P L I F Y I N G E I I X Q
M Q F Q A J F D Q F A G N V Q Q T R L Q
V A U R J U L B C L C A G I F N T L X F
D W R V P M O A S N F I J M X B K I J X
D O Z S V P H S N X K X T N K S N B S I
X C I N M L N H Y O L A K T W M F H Q W
Y V B X L M S R L Q I R O G O J Q P Z H
A I O F Y K L D B K O T A O V R O Z O G
G Y S H N T F Q E I A D R S V A F C B I
V M Y M A Q R E Z L I A K O G T R K R H
V K D Q D P L R I K O P S S P I M T R U
E W M D A B W N L C Y H F K P O Q R Y Q
B O B H Y L P I P S J F W B X E R A W S
M P A V I O E U L A V Q E J R R Q P T B
```

RATIO
SIMPLIFYING
VALUE
PART
WHOLE
TOTAL
PROPORTIONAL
REDUCING
SCALING

Answers

Q1.

12 : 8

Q2.

11 : 14

Q3.

6 : 12

Q4.

Polly works 2 days a week. Sammy works 3 days a week.

Q5.

Henry has 5 gold stickers. Jacob has 7.

Questions 4 and 5 can be anything you want so long as you have used the correct values.

UNDERSTANDING RATIOS

Q6.

```
T R N L C M K F D M C C Y S F C F V I A
C W O Q N Q H Q K Y H Z R D F Q E U U C
S I S S C A L I N G A A E Z M Y X D V R
S D B L A P Q I M R V S D P P N M M O T
I K L E V S H T D R B R U J N M R C N I
S E P Y Q I S N T U N E C G T L S K R F
J U N D S I M P L I F Y I N G E I I X Q
M Q F Q A J F D Q F A G N V Q Q T R L Q
V A U R J U L B C L C A G I F N T L X F
D W R V P M O A S N F I J M X B K I J X
D O Z S V P H S N X K X T N K S N B S I
X C I N M L N H Y O L A K T W M F H Q W
Y V B X L M S R L Q I R O G O J Q P Z H
A I O F Y K L D B K C T A O V R O Z O G
G Y S H N T F Q E I A D R S V A F C B I
V M Y M A Q R E Z L I A K O G T R K R H
V K D Q D P L R I K O P S S P I M T R U
E W M D A B W N L C Y H F K P O G R Y Q
B O B H Y L P I P S J F W B X E R A W S
M P A V I O E U L A V Q E J R R Q R T B
```

HOW ARE YOU GETTING ON?

RATIO OF SHAPES
(RATIOS)

RATIO OF SHAPES

REMEMBER!

A ratio compares one part to another part

OR

It compares one part in relation to the whole thing.

EXAMPLE

Work out the ratio of shaded squares to white squares.

Step 1

Add up the total number of squares.

- There are 24 squares in total.

> Pay attention to what order you put the numbers in. The numbers must represent each part of the question.

Step 2

Next, work out the number of shaded squares, and the number of white squares.

- There are 9 black squares and 15 white squares.

Therefore, the ratio of shaded squares to white squares is 9 : 15.

This can be simplified to 3 : 5.

For more details on simplifying, see the next chapter!

RATIO OF SHAPES

Question Time!

QUESTION 1

How many small balloons are there compared to large balloons?

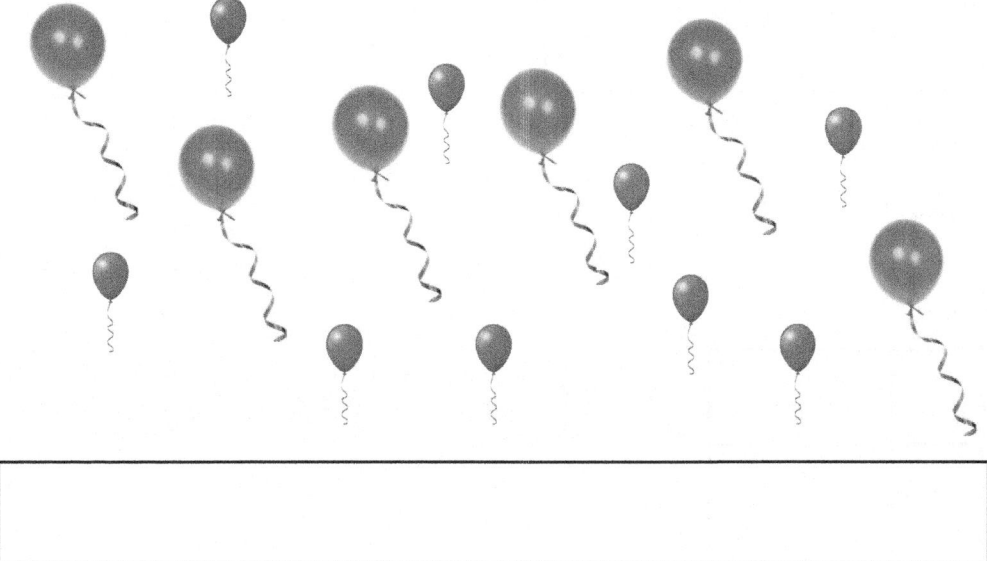

QUESTION 2

Work out the ratio of white triangles to shaded triangles.

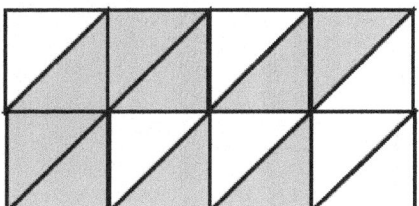

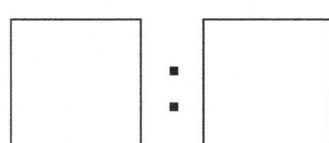

QUESTION 3

Shade in the squares so that the ratio of shaded to white squares is **2 : 6**.

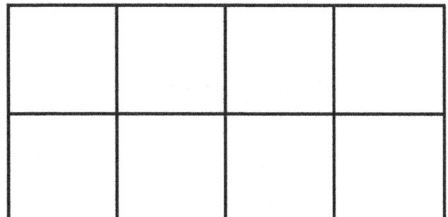

QUESTION 4

Shade in the squares so that the ratio of white to shaded squares is **6 : 3**.

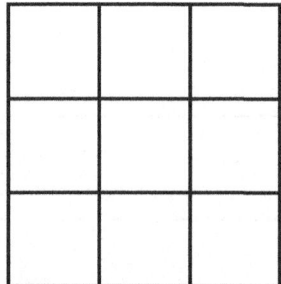

QUESTION 5

Shade in the rectangles so that the ratio of white to shaded rectangles is **7 : 1**.

RATIO OF SHAPES 41

QUESTION 6

Shade in the squares so that the ratio of white to shaded squares is **15 : 5**.

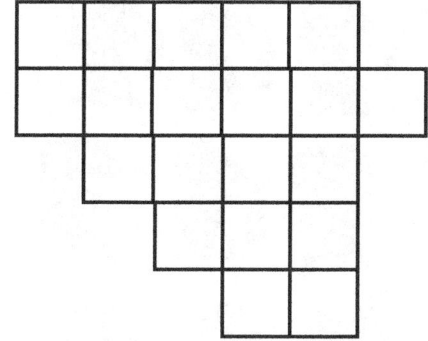

QUESTION 7

Work out the ratio of white triangles to shaded triangles.

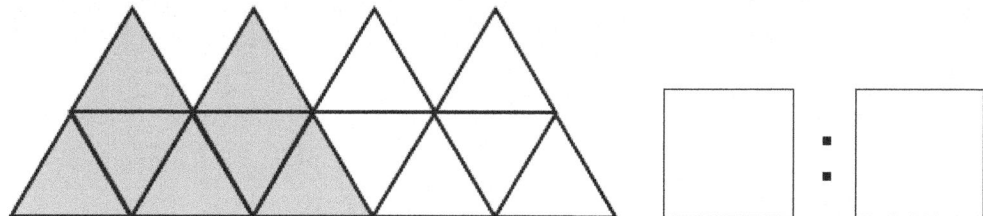

QUESTION 8

Work out the ratio of shaded segments to white segments.

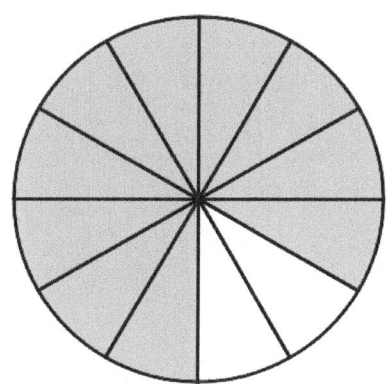

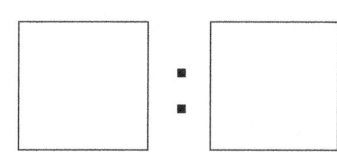

QUESTION 9

Work out the ratio of girls to boys.

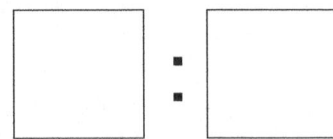

RATIO OF SHAPES

Answers

Q1.

9 : 6 (3 : 2 is also acceptable – see next chapter for details on simplifying ratios)

Q2.

7 : 9

Q3.

For this question, you will need to shade in any two squares.

Q4.

For this question, you will need to shade in any 3 squares.

Q5.

For this question, you will need to shade just 1 rectangle.

Q6.

For this question, you will need to shade in 5 squares.

Q7.

6 : 7

Q8.

10 : 2

Q9.

11 : 10

HOW ARE YOU GETTING ON?

SIMPLIFYING RATIOS
(RATIOS)

SIMPLIFYING RATIOS

Sometimes, a ratio can be 'simplified'.

All this means is that it is made easier to understand, by putting the ratio in smaller numbers, but still representing the same information.

The process of simplifying is quite easy. All you have to do is find a number that both values of the ratio can be divided by.

The ratio will be in its simplest form, when there are no numbers that can be divided into both values of the ratio.

EXAMPLE

Simplify 40 : 60. Write your answer in its simplest form.

Step 1

Both '40' and '60' can be divided by 10.

- If you divide both numbers by 10, you get the ratio: 4 : 6

Step 2

Both '4' and '6' can be divided by 2.

- If you divide both numbers by 2, you would get the ratio: 2 : 3

Step 3

No other numbers can be divided equally into 2 and 3, so 2 : 3 is the simplest form of 40 : 60.

See how the ratios 40 : 60, 4 : 6 and 2 : 3 are all equivalent ratios = they all mean the same thing!

SIMPLIFYING RATIOS

Question Time!

QUESTION 1

Write these ratios in their simplest form.

a) 20 : 5   ☐ : ☐

b) 100 : 75   ☐ : ☐

c) 64 : 32   ☐ : ☐

QUESTION 2

Below there are 10 cards. Each card has a ratio. Match the equivalent boxes from the top row to its simplest ratio in the bottom row.

27 : 15   50 : 5   62 : 34   51 : 34   72 : 48

10 : 1   3 : 2   9 : 5   3 : 2   31 : 17

QUESTION 3

If the statement is true, put a ✓ in the box. If the statement is false, put a ✗ in the box.

a) 9 : 4 is equivalent to 54 : 24.

b) 24 : 12 in its simplest form is 1 : 2.

c) 13 : 10 is already in its simplest form.

d) 150 grams of flour, 50 grams of sugar and 100 grams of butter is used for a cake recipe. In its simplest form, this would be 2 : 1 : 3.

QUESTION 4

Work out the ratio of shaded to unshaded shapes.

Write your answer in its simplest form.

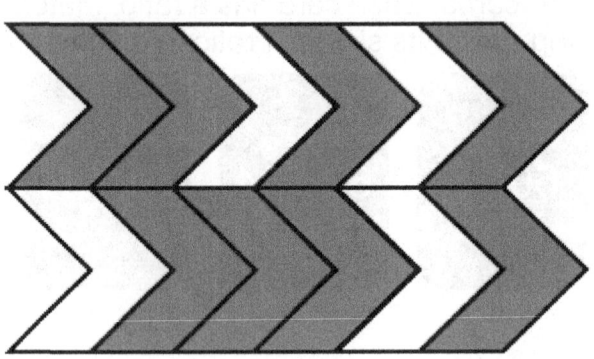

QUESTION 5

A school has organised a school trip to London to see a show.

In total, there are 45 children and 9 adults attending.

Work out the ratio of children to adults attending the trip. Give your answer in its simplest form.

_____

_____

_____

_____

QUESTION 6

Write the following ratios in their simplest form.

a) 120 : 80   b) 148 : 124   c) 36 : 11

_____   _____   _____

d) 84 : 32   e) 300 : 150   f) 268 : 136

_____   _____   _____

QUESTION 7

Below we have provided you with three ratios. For each, write three equivalent ratios.

a) 7 : 3

_____

b) 5 : 2

_____

c) 11 : 13

_____

Answers

Q1.

a) 4 : 1

b) 4 : 3

c) 2 : 1

Q2.

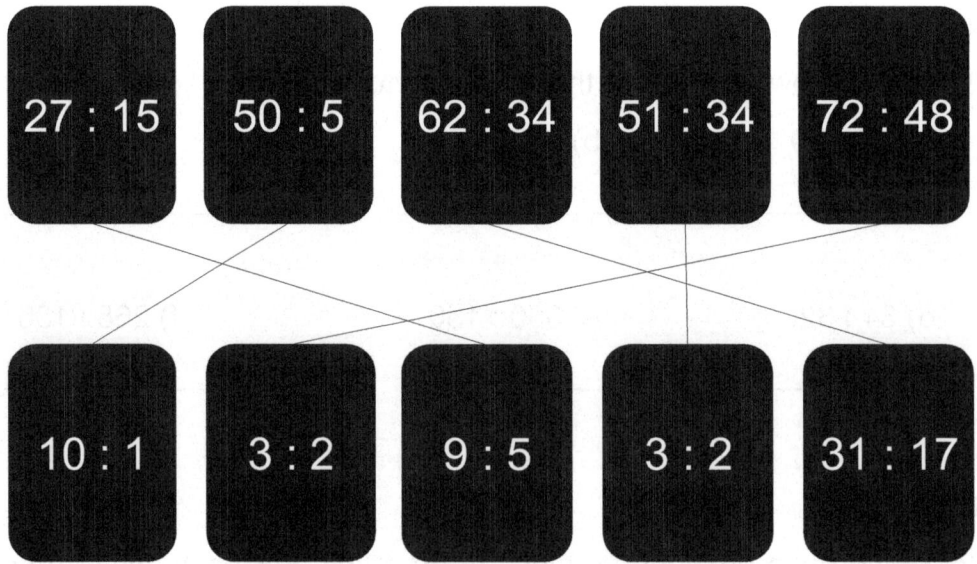

Q3.

a) True

b) False

c) True

d) False

SIMPLIFYING RATIOS

Q4.

8 : 4 (or 2 : 1)

Q5.

5 : 1

- There are 5 children to every 1 adult.
- If there are 45 students on the school trip. That means 5 adults are needed to accompany them.

Q6.

a) 3 : 2

b) 37 : 31

c) 36 : 11

d) 21 : 8

e) 2 : 1

f) 67 : 34

Q7.

a) 14 : 6   21 : 9   28 : 12

b) 10 : 4   15 : 6   20 : 8

c) 22 : 26   33 : 39   44 : 52

HOW ARE YOU GETTING ON?

RATIOS AND SCALING
(RATIOS)

RATIOS AND SCALING

When you're working with ratios, sometimes you might be given the ratio, and then given a size of an actual part.

Your job is to work out the other size, based on the ratio given.

EXAMPLE

Jason and Matthew each have elastic bands in the ratio of 6 : 4.

If Jason has 42 elastic bands, how many elastic bands does Matthew have?

Step 1

First of all, we need to work out how the ratio of 6 (Jason) increases to 42.

$$6 : 4$$
$$42 : ?$$

Step 2

You can multiply the 6 by 7 to give you 42.

Step 3

That means we must multiply the other ratio by 7 to work out how many elastic bands Matthew has.

$$\times 7 \quad 6 : 4 \quad \times 7$$
$$42 : 28$$

REMEMBER

Whatever you do to one part of the ratio, has to be done to the other part of the ratio!

RATIOS AND SCALING 55

Question Time!

QUESTION 1

Abbie has blue and black buttons in the ratio of 3 : 2.

If there are 51 blue buttons, how many black buttons does Abbie have?

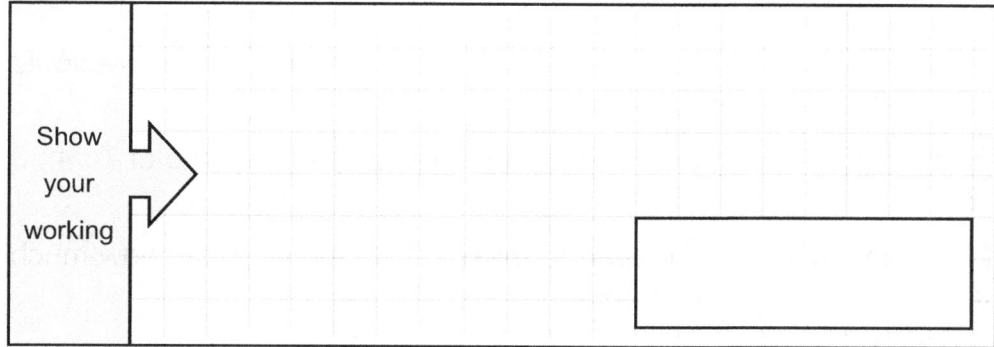

QUESTION 2

Andy is having a BBQ. The only thing he is cooking is burgers and sausages. He cooks these in the ratio of 7 : 8.

If there are 104 sausages, work out how many burgers Andy cooked for his BBQ.

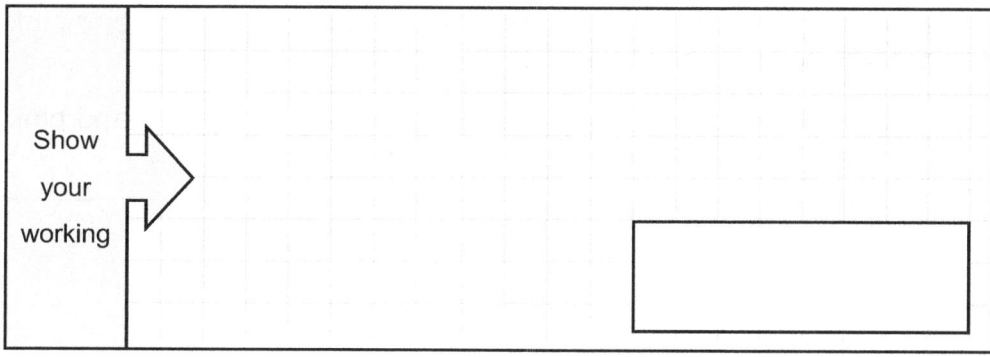

QUESTION 3

Let's make a cake!

To begin, we need to make the cupcake. We need the ingredients flour, butter, sugar and eggs.

To make 1 cake we need the above ingredients in the ratio of 7 : 4 : 3 : 2.

If 42 grams of flour is needed to make 60 cakes, work out how much of each ingredient you will need.

BUTTER _____ (grams)

SUGAR _____ (grams)

EGGS _____ (number of eggs)

QUESTION 4

There are 600 crayons in a box. The ratio of red, blue, green and pink crayons are in the ratio of 4 : 2 : 1 : 5.

If there are 100 blue crayons, work out how many red, green and pink crayons there are in the box.

RATIOS AND SCALING

Answers

Q1.

34

- 51 ÷ 3 = 17
- 17 x 2 = 34
- So there are 51 blue buttons and 34 black buttons.

Q2.

91

- 104 ÷ 8 = 13
- 13 x 7 = 91
- So there are 104 sausages being cooked and 91 burgers for the BBQ.

Q3.

Butter = 24 grams   Sugar = 18 grams   Eggs = 12 eggs

- 42 ÷ 7 = 6
- 6 x 4 = 24 (grams of butter)
- 6 x 3 = 18 (grams of sugar)
- 6 x 2 = 12 (number of eggs)

Q4.

Red = 200   Green = 50   Pink = 250

- 100 blue crayons
- 50 x 4 = 200 red crayons
- 50 x 1 = 50 green crayons
- 50 x 5 = 250 pink crayons

PROPORTIONAL DIVISION
(RATIOS)

PROPORTIONAL DIVISION

Proportional division is very simple to understand.

This is where you will be given a total, and you have to divide that total by the two parts of the ratio.

There are 3 steps that you need to follow in order to work out proportional division correctly.

STEP 1
Add up the two parts of the ratio.

STEP 2
Divide the total by the number of both parts (the number you get after adding both parts of the ratio).

STEP 3
Multiply that number by the number of parts you are trying to work out.

EXAMPLE

Tim and Tom are going to share £800 in the ratio of 13 : 7. How much will Tim's share be?

Step 1

Add up the ratios = 13 + 7 = 20

Step 2

Divide 800 by 20 = 800 ÷ 20 = 40

Step 3

Multiply the 40 by Tim's share (which is 13) = 40 x 13 = £520

PROPORTIONAL DIVISION

Question Time!

QUESTION 1

Vincent and Dave are given £1,200. They have agreed to split the money in the ratio of 2 : 3.

How much money will each person get?

Vincent

___

Dave

___

QUESTION 2

Harrison, Katie and Ryan all work in a restaurant during their summer holidays.

In total, they earn £800 in tips in just 6 weeks.

They decide to split the money in the ratio of the number of hours each person worked. The ratio they split these tips into is 12 : 8 : 20.

Calculate how much each person will receive in tips.

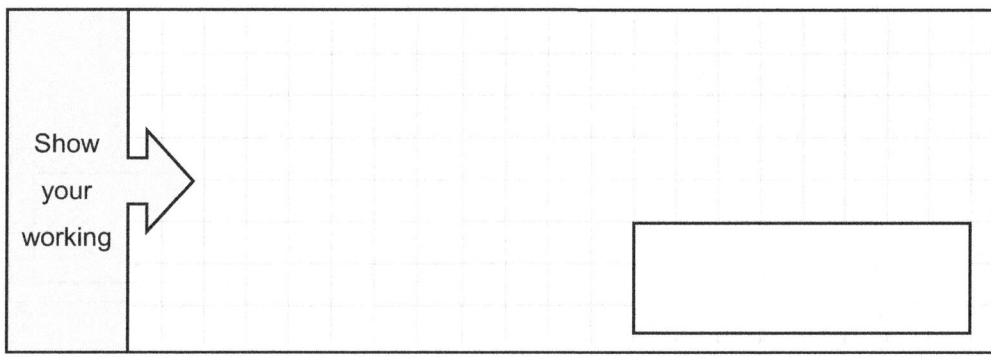

QUESTION 3

Carl wants to do a science experiment. This experiment will take a total of 24 hours. Each stage of the experiment will take a specific amount of time.

He needs to divide his time up in the ratio of 3 : 2 : 4 : 3.

Work out how many hours Carl has to spend on each stage of the science experiment.

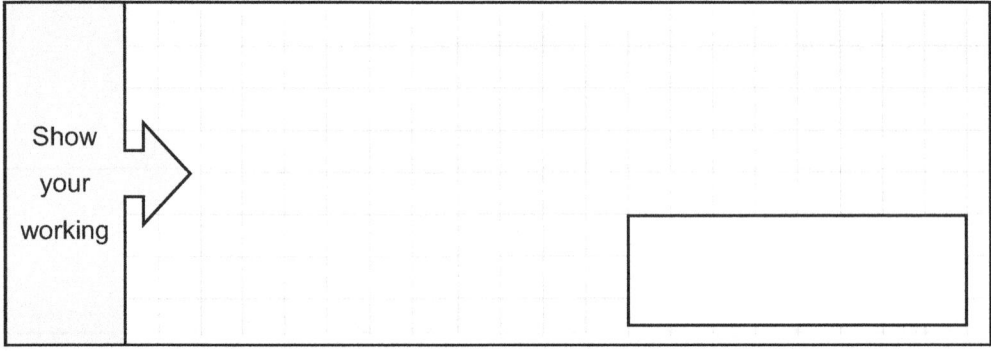

QUESTION 4

William has made a fruit punch. He uses three ingredients: apple juice, orange juice and cranberry juice.

He needs to make a total of 750 ml of fruit punch.

If his recipe for his fruit juice is in the ratio of 11 : 8 : 6, work out how much of each ingredient he will need to make enough fruit punch.

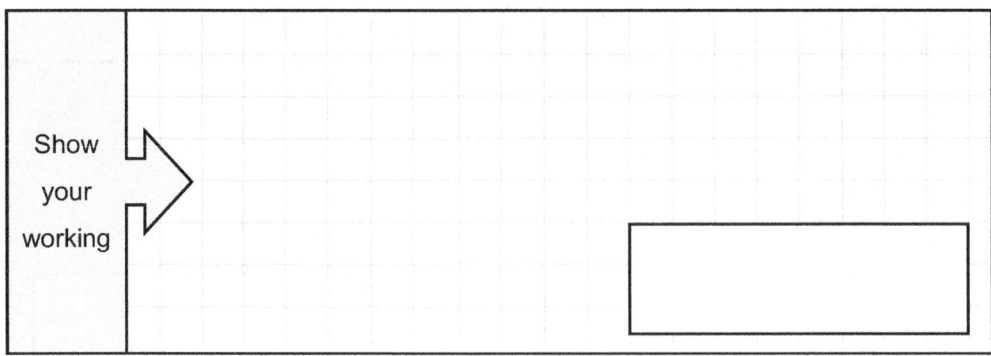

PROPORTIONAL DIVISION

Answers

Q1.

Vincent = £480   Dave = £720

- 2 + 3 = 5
- 1,200 ÷ 5 = 240
- 240 x 2 = £480 for Vincent
- 240 x 3 = £720 for Dave

Q2.

Harrison = £240   Katie = £160   Ryan = £400

- 12 + 8 + 20 = 40
- 800 ÷ 40 = 20
- 20 x 12 = £240 for Harrison
- 20 x 8 = £160 for Katie
- 20 x 20 = £400 for Ryan

Q3.

6 hours   4 hours   8 hours   6 hours

- 3 + 2 + 4 + 3 = 12
- 24 ÷ 12 = 2
- 2 x 3 = 6 hours
- 2 x 2 = 4 hours
- 2 x 4 = 8 hours

- 2 x 3 = 6 hours

Q4.

330 ml apple   240 ml orange   180 ml cranberry

- 11 + 8 + 6 = 25
- 750 ÷ 25 = 30
- 30 x 11 = 330 apple juice
- 30 x 8 = 240 orange juice
- 30 x 6 = 180 cranberry juice

HOW ARE YOU GETTING ON?

DIRECT PROPORTION
(PROPORTION)

DIRECT PROPORTION

Direct proportion is when two quantities increase or decrease in the ratio.

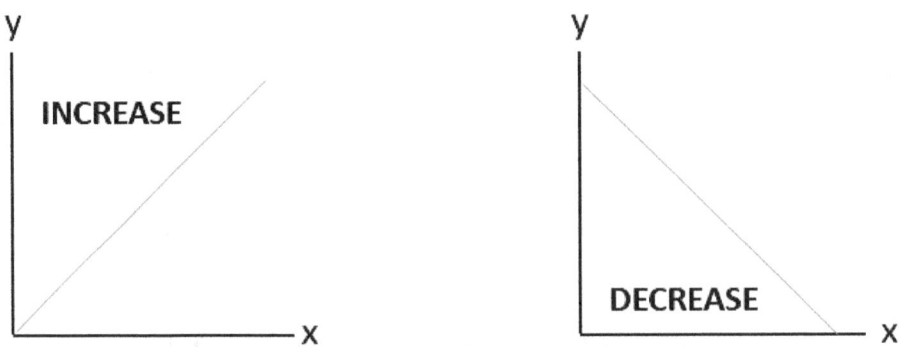

It is relatively simple to work out questions relating to direct proportion.

There is one simple rule that you need to learn to work out direct proportion questions.

RULE
DIVIDE to find one, and then **MULTIPLY** to find all.

EXAMPLE

If 7 sandwiches cost £23.80, how much would it cost for 13 sandwiches?

Step 1

Divide the cost by the number of sandwiches = £23.80 ÷ 7 = £3.40

Step 2

That means 1 sandwich will cost £3.40

Step 3

So, 3.40 x 13 = £44.20

DIRECT PROPORTION

Question Time!

QUESTION 1

Thirteen crayons cost 91p. Find the cost of 34 crayons.

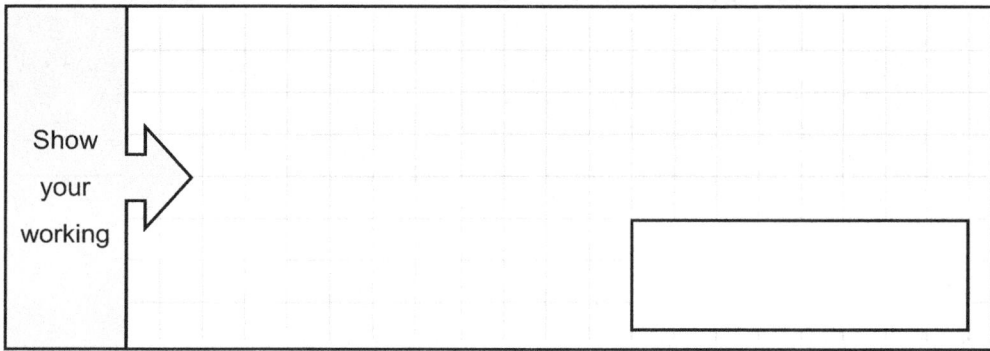

QUESTION 2

If $y = 9$, when $x = 3$, work out the value of x when y is 81.

Show your working

QUESTION 3

4 decorators can decorate 12 rooms in one day.

How many rooms could be decorated if there were 16 decorators?

QUESTION 4

a is directly proportional to b, such that a = 3b.

Work out the value of a when b = 6.

QUESTION 5

a is directly proportional to b. When a = 40 and b = 8:

a) Work out the value of a when b = 10.

---

b) Work out the value of b when a = 48.

---

c) Find an equation for a in terms of b.

QUESTION 6

The cost of carpet increases based on the length.

The cost for a carpet of 4 meters is £360.

Work out the cost of a carpet which is 16 meters in length.

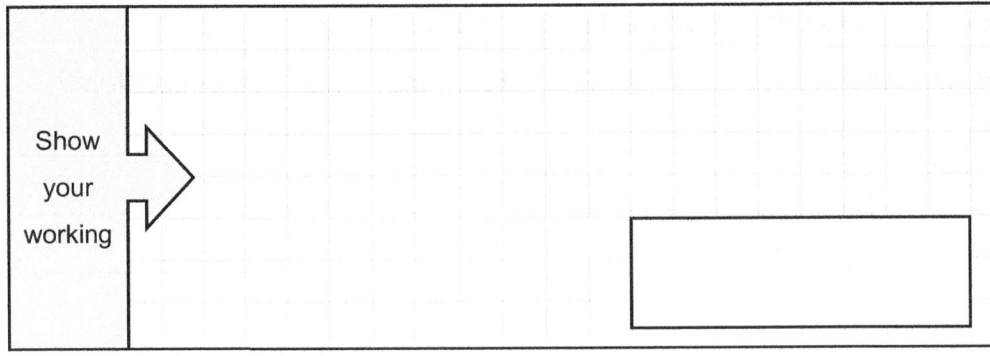

Answers

Q1.

£2.38

- 91 ÷ 13 = 7p
- 7 x 34 = £2.38

Q2.

$x = 27$

- 81 ÷ 9 = 9
- 9 x 3 = 27

Q3.

48

- 12 ÷ 4 = 3
- 3 x 16 = 48

Q4.

- a = 18
- b = 6 x 3 = 18

Q5.

   a) $a = 50$

      ◦ 40 ÷ 8 = 5

      ◦ 5 x 10 = 50

   b) $b = 9.6$

      ◦ 8 ÷ 40 = 0.2

      ◦ 0.2 x 48 = 9.6

   c) $a = 5b$

Q6.

£1,440

- 360 ÷ 4 = £90
- 90 x 16 = £1,440

HOW ARE YOU GETTING ON?

INDIRECT (INVERSE) PROPORTION (PROPORTION)

INDIRECT PROPORTION

Indirect proportion is when one quantity increases as the other decreases, or vice versa.

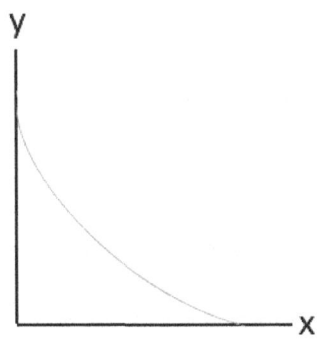

The equation for this is $y = A \div x$

The N being the number value.

Indirect proportion, also known as inverse proportion, is a lot trickier than the chapter just before!

RULE
MULTIPLY to find one, and then **DIVIDE** to find all.

EXAMPLE

It takes 4 chefs 6 hours to prepare and cook a 3-course meal. How long would it take 12 chefs?

Step 1

Multiply the number of chefs (4) by the number of hours (6) = 4 x 6 = 24 hours for 1 chef.

Step 2

Then, divide by 12 to work out how long it would take 12 chefs to cook. = 24 ÷ 12 = 2 hours.

INDIRECT (INVERSE) PROPORTION

Question Time!

QUESTION 1

It takes 3 teachers 12 hours to mark 100 exam papers.

How long will it take to mark 100 exam papers if 4 teachers marked the papers?

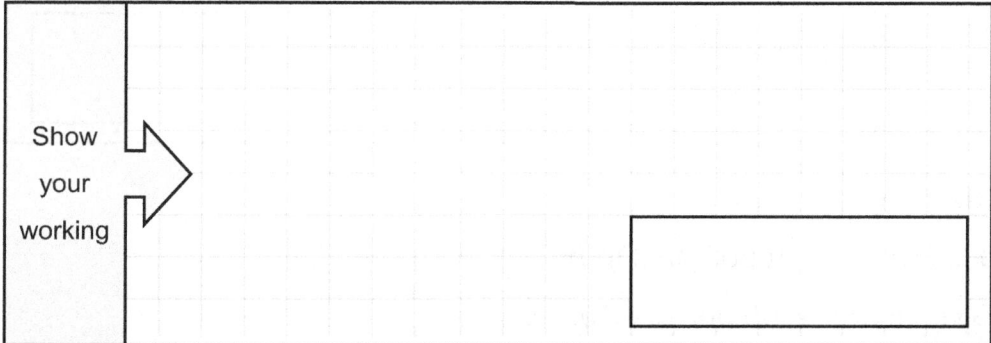

Show your working

QUESTION 2

a is inversely proportional to b.

If $a = 50$ and $b = 250$, calculate the value of b when $a = 80$.

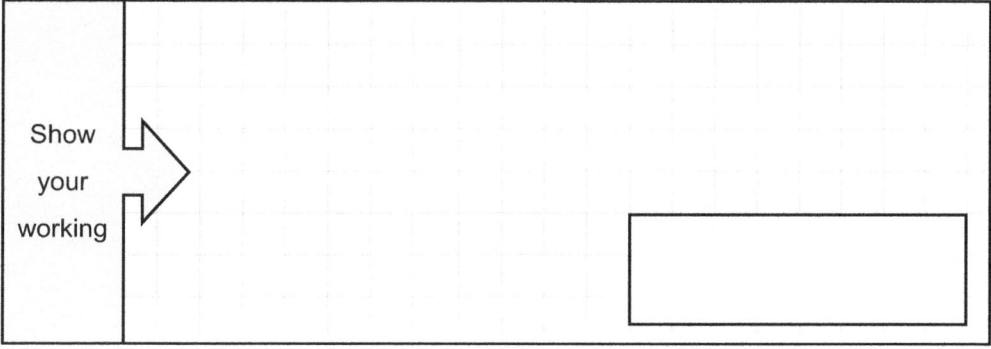

Show your working

QUESTION 3

It takes 6 people to dig up the entire garden in 18 days.

Assuming that everyone is working at the same pace, how long would it take 2 people to dig up the garden?

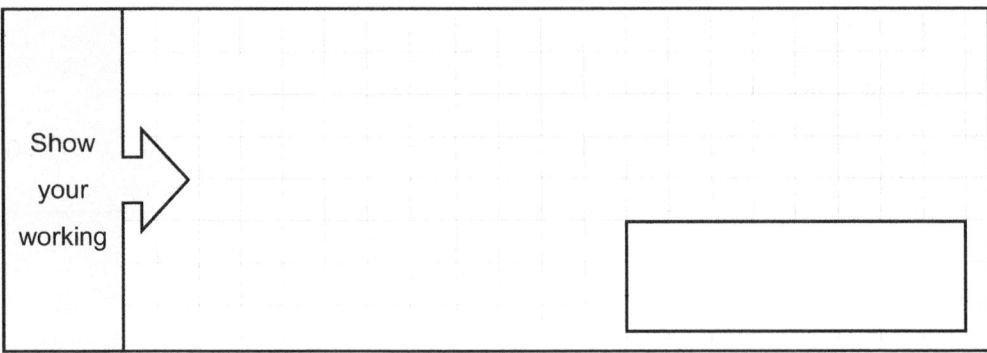

QUESTION 4

a is inversely proportional to b^2.

Given that a = 4.5 and b = 15:

Find an equation for a in terms of b.

_____
_____
_____

INDIRECT (INVERSE) PROPORTION

Answers

Q1.

9 hours

- 3 x 12 = 36 hours for 1 teacher
- 36 ÷ 4 = 9 hours

Q2.

$b = 160$

- 80 ÷ 50 = 1.6
- 1.6 x 100 = 160

Q3.

54 days

- 6 x 18 = 108 days for 1 person
- 108 ÷ 2 = 54 days for 2 people

Q4.

$225/b^2$

HOW ARE YOU GETTING ON?

PERCENTAGE INCREASE
(PERCENTAGE CHANGE)

PERCENTAGE INCREASE

INCREASE = New Number − Original Number

Divide the difference by the original number

Multiply by 100

EXAMPLE

A suit before Christmas cost £60.00. Its price now is £180.00. Work out the percentage increase of the suit.

Step 1

Subtract the original cost from the new cost.

- 180 − 60 = 120

Step 2

Divide the increase by the original number.

- 120 ÷ 60 = 2

Step 3

Multiply this by 100.

- 2 x 100 = 200

So, the suit's price increased by 200%.

PERCENTAGE INCREASE

ALTERNATIVE METHOD 1

A bed has increased in price by 25%. The original price for the bed was £110.

What is the new price of the bed?

Step 1

Turn the percentage into a decimal.

- 25% = 25 ÷ 100 = 0.25

Step 2

Multiply the original number by the decimal.

- 0.25 x £110 = £27.50

Step 3

Because you are working out the percentage **increase**, you will add this to the original price.

- £110 + 27.50 = £137.50

ALTERNATIVE METHOD 2

A sofa has increased in price by 40%. The original price for the bed was £340.

What is the new price of the sofa?

Step 1

Turn the percentage into a decimal.

- 40% = 1 + 0.40 = 1.40 (if you were finding the decrease, you would subtract)

Step 2

Multiply the original number by the decimal.

- 1.40 x £340 = £476

REMEMBER

A percentage increase, as a decimal, will be above 1, and a percentage decrease will be below 1.

PERCENTAGE INCREASE 81

Question Time!

QUESTION 1

Below shows two different companies with key information.

Company	Company Profit (Annual) (£)	Cost to buy company (£)	Number of employees
A	15,000	18,000	6
B	26,000	24,000	11

a) If company A's annual profit increased by 20% in the next year, what would their annual company profit be for that year?

Show your working

b) What would company B's annual profit be next year if it increased by 40%?

Show your working

QUESTION 2

In July, Ryan worked a total of 40 hours.

In August, he worked 46.5 hours.

By what percentage did Ryan's working hours increase in August?

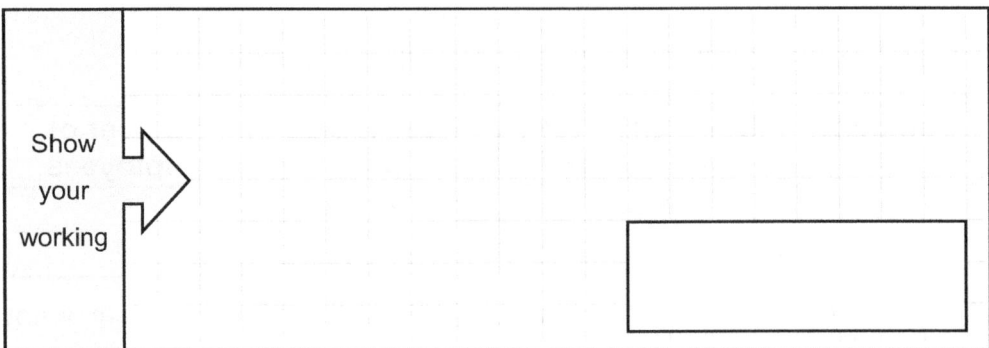

QUESTION 3

Pupils who succeeded in getting a Science GCSE at Grade C or above were analysed from 2005 to 2010.

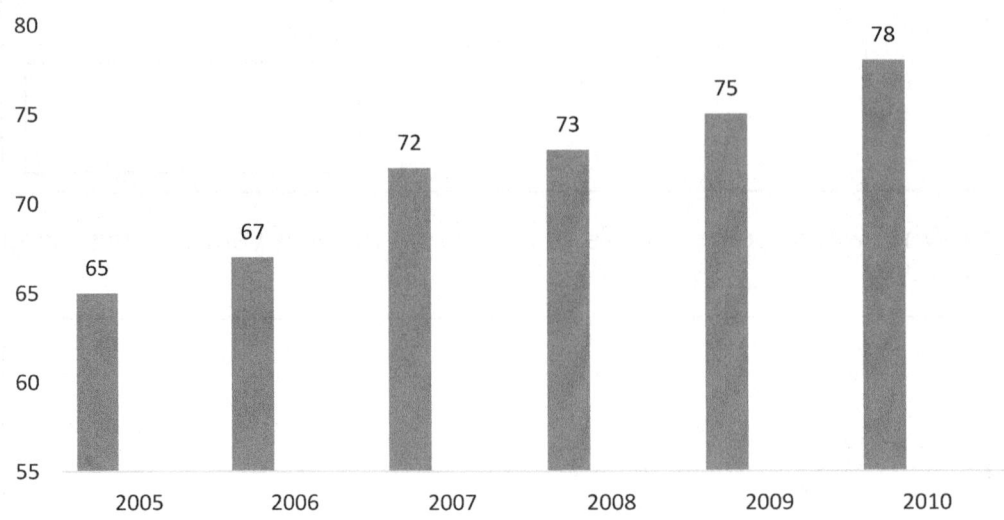

The percentage increase from 2005 and 2010 is 20%. True or false?

PERCENTAGE INCREASE

QUESTION 4

Below is a bar chart showing regional sweet sales in supermarkets, in 2014. The numbers are in hundreds of thousands.

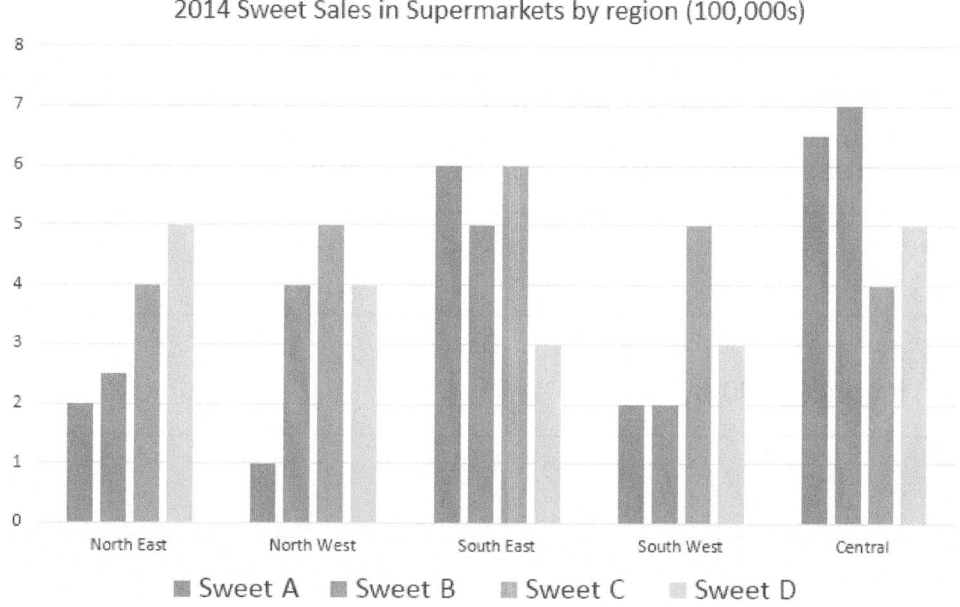

a) What was the total percentage increase for Sweet A, when comparing North East and South East regional supermarket sales?

A	B	C	D
150%	50%	250%	200%

b) What was the percentage increase between sweet A and sweet B for North West?

A	B	C	D
50%	25%	300%	350%

QUESTION 5

Increase the following numbers by the percentage shown.

a) Increase 90 by 25%

b) Increase 150 by 60%

c) Increase 300 by 120%

d) Increase 700 by 80%

e) Increase 50 by 5%

f) Increase 97 by 150%

PERCENTAGE INCREASE

Answers

Q1.

   a) £18,000

       ○ 20% increase = 1.20

       ○ 15,000 x 1.20 = £18,000

   b) £36,400

       ○ 40% increase = 1.40

       ○ 26,000 x 1.40 = £36,400

Q2.

16.25%

- 46.5 − 40 = 6.5
- 6.5 ÷ 40 = 0.1625
- 0.1625 x 100 = 16.25%

Q3.

True

- 78 − 65 = 13
- 13 ÷ 65 = 0.2
- 0.2 x 100 = 20%

Q4.

a) D = 200%
- 600,000 - 200,000 = 400,000
- 400,000 ÷ 200,000 = 2
- 2 x 100 = 200%

b) C = 300%
- 400,000 − 100,000 = 300,000
- 300,000 ÷ 100,000 = 3
- 3 x 100 = 300%

Q5.

a) 112.5
- 25% increase = 1.25
- 1.25 x 90 = 112.5

b) 240
- 60% increase = 1.60
- 1.60 x 150 = 240

c) 660
- 120% increase = 2.20
- 2.20 x 300 = 660

PERCENTAGE INCREASE

d) 1,260
- 80% increase = 1.80
- 1.80 x 700 = 1,260

e) 52.5
- 5% increase = 1.05
- 1.05 x 50 = 52.5

f) 242.5
- 150% increase = 2.50
- 2.50 x 97 = 242.5

HOW ARE YOU GETTING ON?

PERCENTAGE DECREASE
(PERCENTAGE CHANGE)

PERCENTAGE DECREASE

DECREASE = Original Number – New Number

Divide the difference by the original number

Multiply by 100

EXAMPLE

A house was bought for £150,000. But, it has been valuated this year, and is now worth £80,000.

Work out the percentage decrease between the two prices.

Step 1

Work out the difference between the two numbers.

- 150,000 – 80,000 = 70,000

Step 2

Divide the decrease by the original number.

- 70,000 ÷ 150,000 = 0.46666…

Step 3

Multiply this by 100.

- 0.46666… x 100 = 46.67 (to two decimal places)

PERCENTAGE DECREASE

ALTERNATIVE METHOD 1

A bed has decreased in price by 25%. The original price for the bed was £110.

What is the new price of the bed?

Step 1

Turn the percentage into a decimal.

- 25% = 25 ÷ 100 = 0.25

Step 2

Multiply the original number by the decimal.

- 0.25 x £110 = £27.50

Step 3

Because you are working out the percentage decrease, you will subtract this from the original price.

- £110 - 27.50 = £82.50

ALTERNATIVE METHOD 2

A sofa has decreased in price by 40%. The original price for the bed was £340.

What is the new price of the sofa?

Step 1

Turn the percentage into a decimal.

- 40% = 1 - 0.40 = 1.60. (You are subtracting because you are working out the decreased value).

Step 2

Multiply the original number by the decimal.

- 0.60 x £340 = £204

REMEMBER

A percentage increase, as a decimal, will be above 1, and a percentage decrease will be below 1.

PERCENTAGE DECREASE 93

Question Time!

QUESTION 1

A shop sells a high-tech computer system. The original price of the computer system was £1,400. There is a discount for this product of 30% off.

Work out the new price of the high-tech computer system.

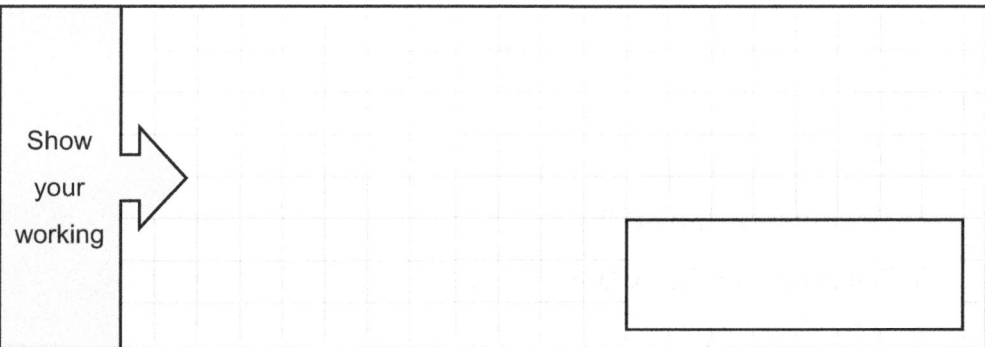

QUESTION 2

Work out the missing gaps in the table.

ORIGINAL PRICE	DISCOUNT	NEW PRICE
£400	15% off	
£1,500		£450
£98	5% off	
£120	11% off	

QUESTION 3

ACROSS

1) The price of a dress was originally £150. It's now been discounted to the price of £90. What percentage decrease is this?

4) What is 30% of 50?

6) A car originally cost £2,000. Its new price is £1500. What percentage decrease is this?

7) A robot was has been reduced by 25%. If the cost of the robot was originally £80, how much is the robot now?

DOWN

2) 90% decrease of 1,000 is?

3) Decrease 200 by 60%

5) Decrease 4,000 by 98%

PERCENTAGE DECREASE

QUESTION 4

Decrease the following numbers by the percentage shown.

a) Decrease 300 by 25%

b) Decrease 170 by 20%

c) Decrease 3,500 by 60%

d) Decrease 75 by 5%

e) Decrease 120 by 12%

f) Decrease 10,000 by 89%

Answers

Q1.

£980

- 30% decrease = 0.70
- 0.70 x 1,400 = £980

Q2.

ORIGINAL PRICE	DISCOUNT	NEW PRICE
£400	15% off	£340
£1,500	70% off	£450
£98	5% off	£93.10
£120	11% off	£106.80

Q3.

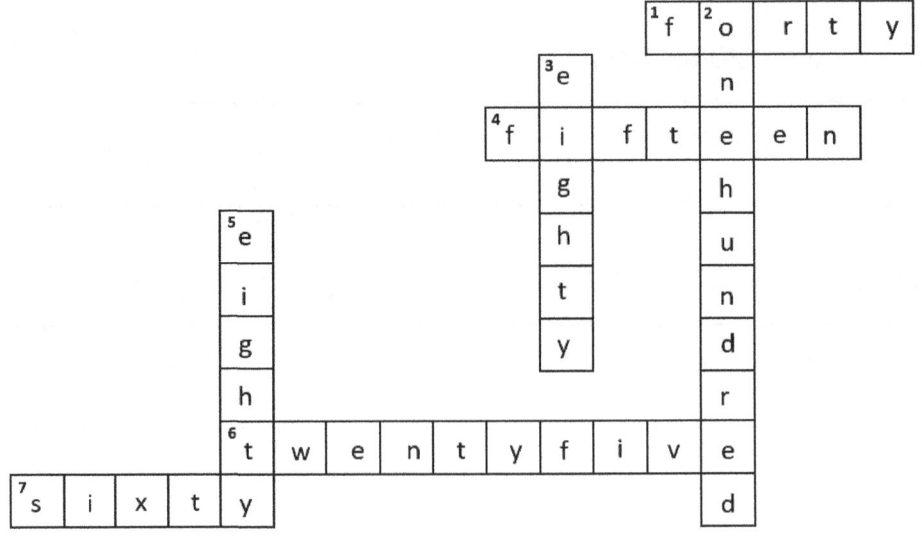

PERCENTAGE DECREASE

Q4.

a) 225
- 25% decrease = 0.75
- 0.75 x 300 = 225

b) 136
- 20% decrease = 0.80
- 0.80 x 170 = 136

c) 1,400
- 60% decrease = 0.40
- 0.40 x 3,500 = 1,400

d) 71.25
- 5% decrease = 0.95
- 0.95 x 75 = 71.25

e) 105.6
- 12% decrease = 0.88
- 0.88 x 120 = 105.6

f) 1,100
- 89% decrease = 0.11
- 0.11 x 10,000 = 1,100

HOW ARE YOU GETTING ON?

ADDING INTEREST
(PERCENTAGE CHANGE)

ADDING INTEREST

Interest is a percentage of the total amount. Usually interest is added once a year (like banks do!)

EXAMPLE

Harry has been at the same bank for 3 years, He recently added £5,000 to his account. His account adds 3% basic interest each year.

How much interest does Harry earn in 6 years?

Step 1

First, you need to work out how much interest is added per year:

- 3% = 3 ÷ 100 = 0.03

Step 2

Next, using the decimal, work out how much interest this is based on the amount:

- 0.03 x 5,000 = £150

Step 3

Multiply this interest by the number of years:

- £150 x 6 = £900

So, Harry will earn £900 in 6 years, based on the amount added to his account.

ADDING INTEREST

Question Time!

QUESTION 1

How much interest is earned on £268 at 10% for eight years?

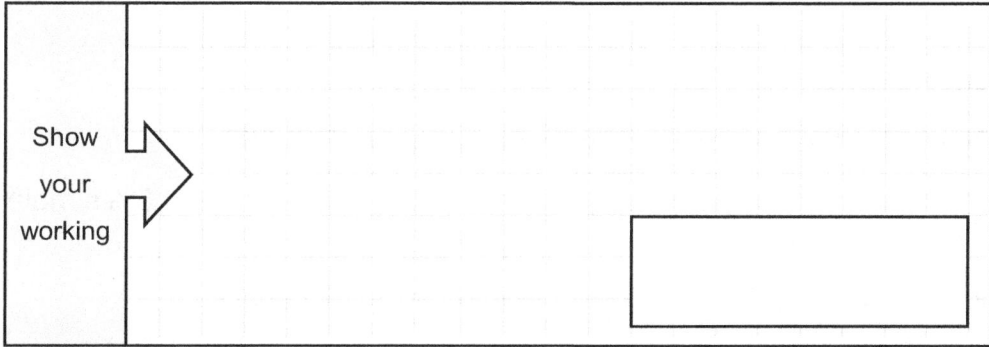

QUESTION 2

You invest £500 at an interest rate of 5%. How much money, in total, will you have after 4 years?

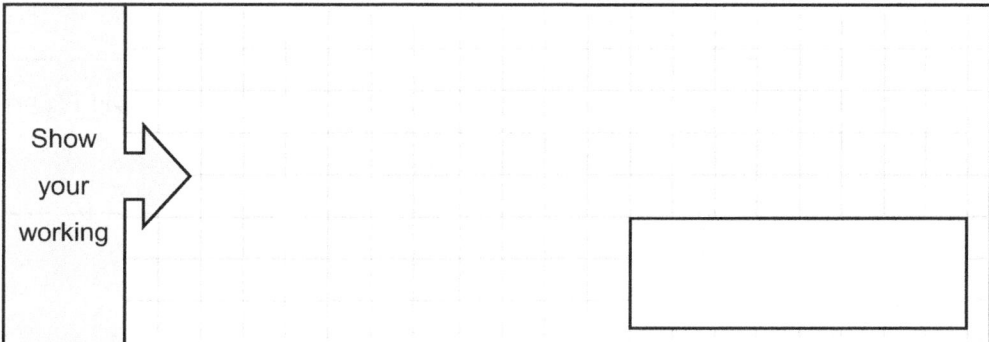

QUESTION 3

For the following statements, circle whether they are **true** or **false**.

a) If you invested £100 with an interest rate of 8%, you would have £432 after 4 years.

TRUE / FALSE

b) If you invested £950 with an interest rate of 12% per year, you would earn £114 on top of your investment.

TRUE / FALSE

c) £1,200 is invested in a bank account which pays a 2% simple interest per year. You will have more than £1,500 after 5 years.

TRUE / FALSE

QUESTION 4

Ryan wins the lottery. His winnings amount to £45,000.

He decided to put this money into an account which pays a 5% simple interest per year.

He aims to keep the money in the account for 15 years.

    a) Based on the information above, work out how much interest Ryan will receive per year.

_____

    b) How much interest, in total, will Ryan receive after the 15 years?

_____

    c) Including his winnings, and interest, how much money will Ryan have at the end of the 15 years?

_____

ADDING INTEREST

Answers

Q1.

£214.40

- 268 ÷ 100 = 2.68
- 2.68 x 10 = £26.80 for 1 year
- 8 years = 26.80 x 8 = £214.40

Q2.

£600

- 5% interest on £500 = 500 ÷ 100 x 5 = 25
- 25 x 4 = £100
- 500 + 100 = £600

Q3.

a) If you invested £100 with an interest rate of 8%, you would have £432 after 4 years.

FALSE

b) If you invested £950 with an interest rate of 12% per year, you would earn £114 on top of your investment.

TRUE

c) £1,200 is invested in a bank account which pays a 2% simple interest per year. You will have more than £1,500 after 5 years.

FALSE

Q4.

   a) £2,250

      - 45,000 ÷ 100 x 5 = £2,250

   b) £33,750

      - 2,250 x 15 = £33,750

   c) £78,750

      - 45,000 + 33,750 = £78,750

HOW ARE YOU GETTING ON?

CHANGE IN VALUE
(PERCENTAGE CHANGE)

FINDING THE CHANGE IN VALUE

PERCENTAGE CHANGE = $\frac{\text{'Change'}}{\text{Original}} \times 100$

EXAMPLE 1

The price of a car increases from £6,000 to £15,000.

Work out the percentage increase.

Step 1

First of all, subtract the original number from the new price:

- 15,000 - 6,000 = 9,000

Step 2

Next, use the formula to work out the percentage increase:

- Percentage increase = $\frac{9000}{6000} \times 100 = 150\%$

REMEMBER

Pay attention to whether you are working out the percentage increase or percentage decrease.

CHANGE IN VALUE

EXAMPLE 2

The price of a house reduces from £250,000 to £120,000

Work out the percentage loss on this house.

Step 1

First of all, subtract the new number from the original price:

- 250,000 − 120,000 = 130,000

Step 2

Next, use the formula to work out the percentage decrease:

- Percentage decrease = $\dfrac{130,000}{250,000} \times 100 = 52\%$

REMEMBER

Pay attention to whether you are working out the percentage increase or percentage decrease.

ACTIVITY TIME!

A company was once worth £140,000.

It is now worth £300,000.

Work out the profit, as a percentage.

WORK OUT THE ORIGINAL VALUE

Sometimes, you may be required to work out the ORIGINAL number, based on the new value and the percentage change.

There are two methods you can use to work out the original value.

METHOD 1
DIVIDE for 1, then MULTIPLY to find 100%

EXAMPLE

The price of a motorbike decreases in price by 10% to £9,000.

Work out what the motorbike's value was **before** the decrease.

Step 1

A decrease of 10% means that £9,000 represents 90% of the original value.

Step 2

Divide value by 90 to find 1%

- £9,000 ÷ 90 = £100

Step 3

Now, multiply the value by 100.

- 100 x 100 = 10,000

So, the original price of the motorbike was £10,000.

REMEMBER

A good way to check to see whether you have the correct answer is to put your answer back into the question and see whether it works.

(10,000 x 0.9 = 9,000)

CHANGE IN VALUE

METHOD 2
Find the **MULTIPLIER** and then **DIVIDE** the **NEW** value by the multiplier

EXAMPLE

The price of a house increases by 60% to £180,000.

Work out the original price of the house.

Step 1

Work out the multiplier:

- 60% increase = 1 + 0.60 = 1.60

Step 2

Finally, divide the new value by the multiplier, in order to work out the original value:

- 180,000 ÷ 1.60 = £112,500

So, the original price of the house was £112,500.

REMEMBER

A good way to check to see whether you have the correct answer is to put your answer back into the question and see whether it works.

(112,500 x 1.60 = 180,000)

ACTIVITY TIME!

A car increases in value by 15% to £12,000.

Can you work out the original price of the car?

QUESTION 1

An antique has been priced before auction.

The price is estimated to be worth £15,000.

At auction, the antique sold for £45,000.

What is the percentage increase of the value of this antique?

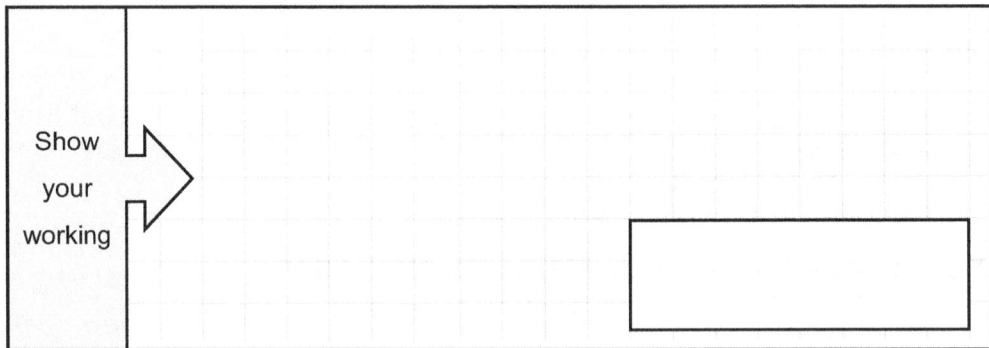

QUESTION 2

A sports player's annual income decreases from £800,000 to £500,000.

Work out the percentage loss of the sports player's annual income.

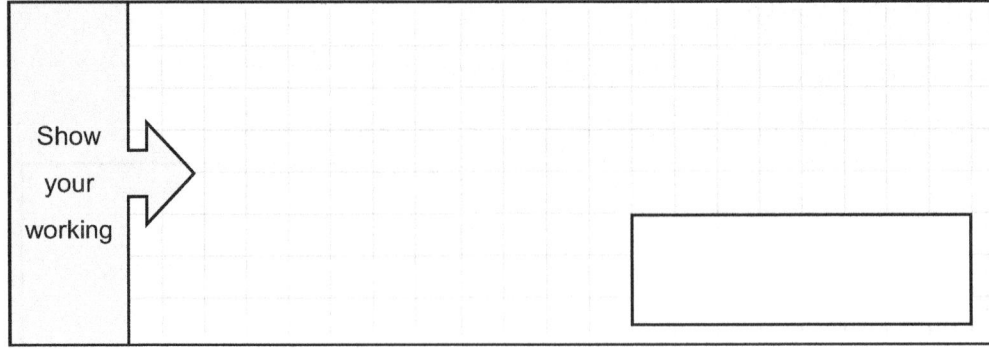

CHANGE IN VALUE

QUESTION 3

Below is a table of a list of company employees and their wages across three years.

NAME	2013	2014	2015	2016
Arnold	£32,000	£30,000	£28,000	£40,000
Eric	£12,000	£10,000	£16,000	£12,000
Petunia	£15,000	£19,000	£25,000	£22,000
Ursula	£30,000	£20,000	£28,000	£35,000

a) Work out the percentage increase for Arnold's wages between 2015 and 2016. Write your answer to 2 decimal places.

Show your working

b) Ursula's wages decreased between 2013 and 2014. What was the percentage decrease? Write your answer to 2 decimal places.

Show your working

c) Work out the percentage increase of Petunia's wages between 2014 and 2015. Write your answer to 2 decimal places.

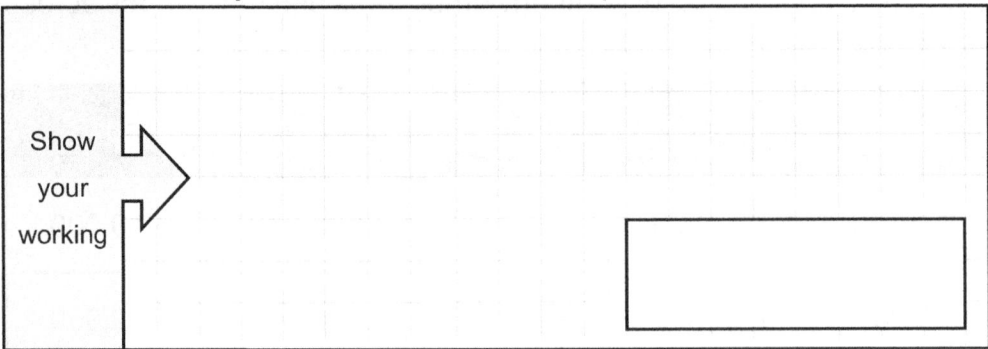

d) Eric's wages increase by what percentage between 2014 and 2015?

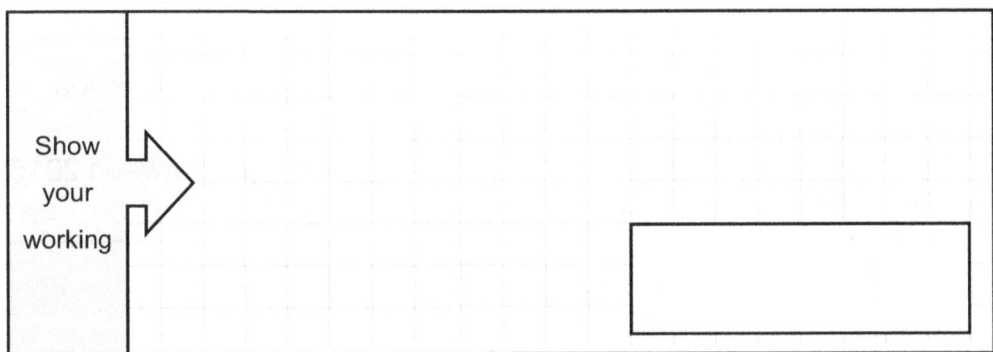

QUESTION 4

The value of a mansion decreases in value by 20% to £800,000.

Find the value of the mansion <u>before</u> the decreased value.

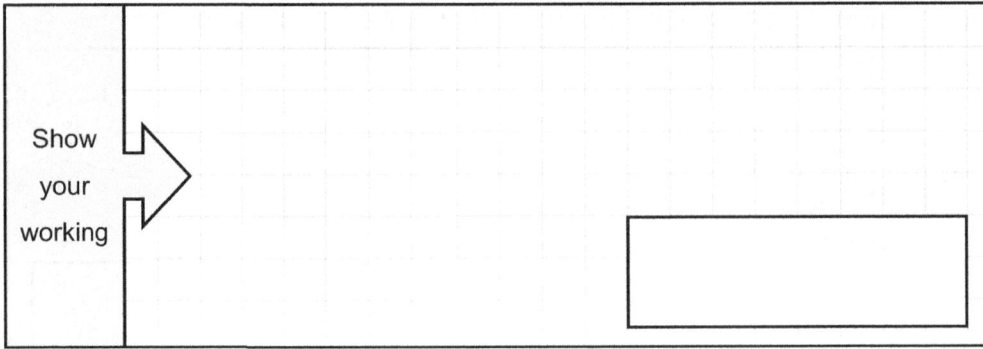

CHANGE IN VALUE

QUESTION 5

The estimated price of a wedding increased in value by 60% to £28,000.

What was the original price estimated for the wedding?

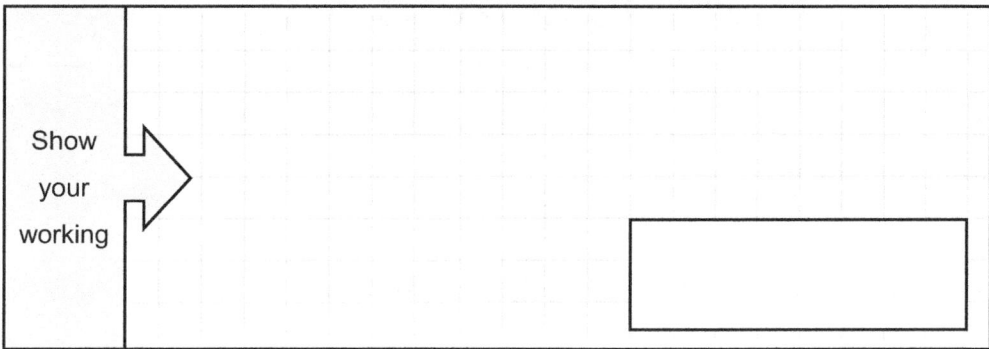

Show your working

QUESTION 6

Complete the wordsearch. These words are all important to percentage change.

```
R U W L B E Y D U W A O D L J M S W H M
L K C I U L P E V N Z S L O L Z B K K G
E B Z L M R C C I L Y G I S B Q B X F D
O E A R Y P L R M E M H W S D S S C I A
F V M G R X P E R C E N T A G E R S C W
G Z A O I U A A Y W C N M H K P C H I F
S C F Z J L N S J I I X N I S O A S B H
A I C L Z O J E R Y O Q W R U N D P F A
T R J R U P U Q J Z A Z M N G L F R I M
D H M R E I H I I J T C T E X S Z F F M
M Y V R U E N R Q L H R S O O X F Y R P
W I E A E I M J P D H U H I N E T G J I
A E R R V J L Y Z W I T C C U C R S C G
E S L R E I L P I T L U M J A J H R V F
L T U B V E S T N U O M A M L G G R O O
T K T G S B N L N Z V A H N P U K M D R
L E N X Z K Z N Y I P K N B Y B R R M M
K H M N D N H R A X C E S A E R C N I U
G J A T T S E R E T N I R D W F K Q X L
E S E B X I M C S X H V L N S P V Z B A
```

PERCENTAGE
CHANGE
INCREASE
DECREASE
VALUE
MULTIPLIER
INTEREST
AMOUNT
PROFIT
LOSS
ERROR
DISCOUNT
FORMULA

Answers

Q1.

200% increase

- £45,000 - £15,000 = £30,000
- Percentage increase = $\frac{30,000}{15,000}$ x 100 = 200%

Q2.

37.5% decrease

- 800,000 − 500,000 = 300,000
- Percentage decrease = $\frac{300,000}{800,000}$ x 100 = 37.5%

Q3.

a) 42.86%
- 40,000 − 28,000 = 12,000
- Percentage increase = $\frac{12,000}{28,000}$ x 100 = 42.857
- To 2 decimal places = 42.86%

b) 33.33%
- 30,000 − 20,000 = 10,000
- Percentage decrease = $\frac{10,000}{30,000}$ x 100 = 33.333
- To 2 decimal places = 33.33%

c) 31.58%

- 25,000 − 19,000 = 6,000
- Percentage increase = $\frac{6,000}{19,000}$ x 100 = 31.58%

d) 60%

- 16,000 − 10,000 = 6,000
- Percentage increase = $\frac{6,000}{10,000}$ x 100 = 60%

Q4.

£1,000,000

- The multiplier = 20% = 1 − 0.2 = 0.8
- 800,000 ÷ 0.8 = 1,000,000

Q5.

£17,500

The multiplier = 60% = 1 + 0.60 = 1.60

28,000 ÷ 1.60 = 17,500

Q6.

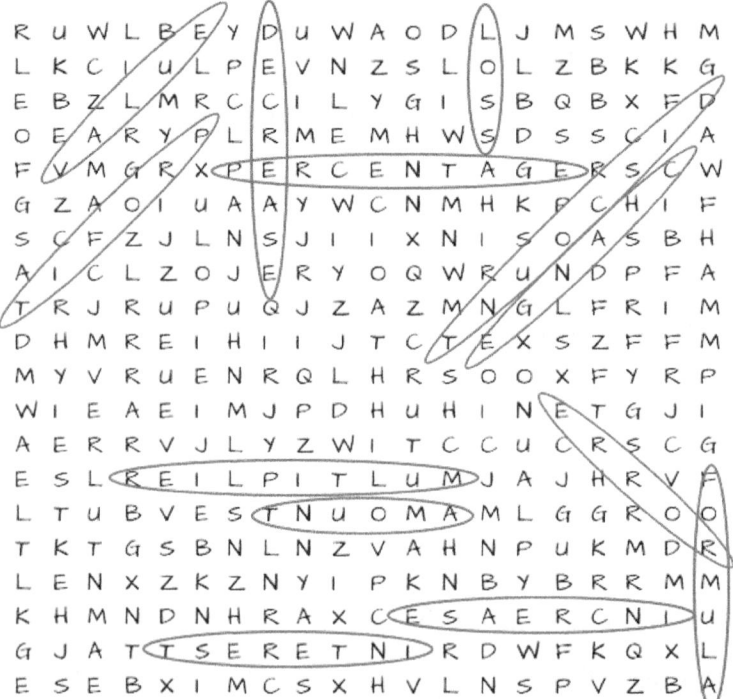

METRIC AND IMPERIAL UNITS

METRIC AND IMPERIAL UNITS

METRIC and IMPERIAL units are types of measurements.

METRIC UNITS	IMPERIAL UNITS
LENGTH mm, cm, m, km	**LENGTH** inches, yards, feet, miles
AREA mm^2, cm^2, m^2, km^2	**AREA** square inches, square feet, square miles
VOLUME mm^3, cm^3, m^3, ml, litres	**VOLUME** pints, cubic inches, cubic feet, gallons
MASS (WEIGHT) g, kg, tonnes	**MASS (WEIGHT)** ounces, pounds, stones, tons
SPEED km/h, m/s	**SPEED** mph

METRIC CONVERSIONS

- 1 cm = 10 mm
- 1 m = 100 cm
- 1 km = 1000 m
- 1 kg = 1000 g
- 1 tonne = 1000 kg
- 1 litre = 1000 ml
- 1 litre = 1000 cm^3
- 1 cm^3 = 1 ml

Learn these off by heart!

METRIC AND IMPERIAL UNITS 119

IMPERIAL CONVERSIONS

- 1 foot = 12 inches
- 1 yard = 3 feet
- 1 gallon = 8 pints
- 1 stone = 14 pounds
- 1 pound = 16 ounces

Learn these off by heart!

METRIC-IMPERIAL CONVERSIONS!

You should try to learn as many of these as you can:

- 1 inch ≈ 2.54 cm
- 1 kg ≈ 2.2 pounds
- 1 foot ≈ 30 cm
- 1 litre ≈ 1.75 pints
- 1 gallon ≈ 4.5 litres
- 1 mile ≈ 1.6 km

The symbol '≈' means 'approximately' or 'nearly equals to'

HOW TO CONVERT

Step 1

Work out the **conversion factor.**

Step 2

Use the conversion factor to work out whether you need to multiply or divide.

Step 3

Do the calculation!

EXAMPLE

An animal is measured as being 150 cm in height.

How tall is the animal in meters?

Step 1

Work out the conversion factor:

- 1 m = 100 cm
- So, the conversion factor is 100.

Step 2

Work out whether you need to multiply or divide:

- There are more centimetres than metres, so you should divide:
- 150 ÷ 100 = 1.5 metres

EXAMPLE

An object has a width of 20 inches.

Work this out in centimetres.

Step 1

Work out the conversion factor:

- 1 inch = 2.54 centimetres
- So, the conversion factor is 2.54.

Step 2

Work out whether you need to multiply or divide:

- We are converting inches into centimetres, so you should multiply
- 20 x 2.54 = 50.8 cm

METRIC AND IMPERIAL UNITS

CONVERSION GRAPHS

The best way to understand conversion graphs is by example. Take a look at the graph below.

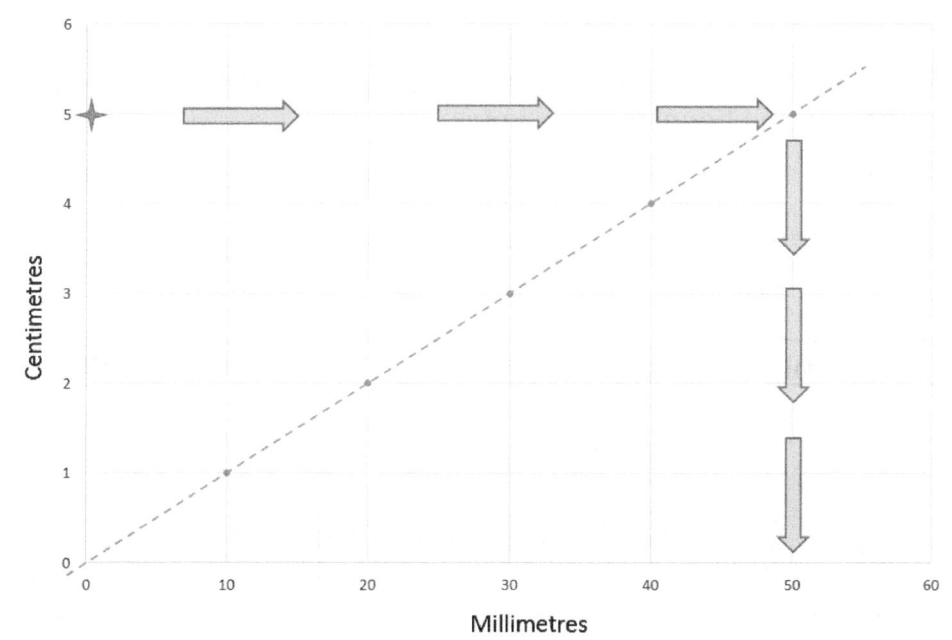

1. The star shape is the value we are starting with (5 centimetres).

2. Working along the horizontal line (the direction in which the arrows are going), you need to keep going until you reach the diagonal striped line.

3. Once you reach the diagonal line, stop. You then need to change direction and continue vertically (the direction in which the next set of arrows are going).

4. You will then reach the bottom of the chart, which you will then be able to read off the conversion value.

5. In this case, it is 50 millimetres. So, 5 centimetres can be converted to (i.e. is the same as), 50 millimetres.

Question Time!

QUESTION 1

Using the following columns, place the words under the correct column. The first one has been done for you.

~~Kilograms~~   Litres   Metres   Grams   Centimetres   Pounds   Kilometres   Inches   Millilitres   Millimetres

Length	Weight	Capacity/Volume
	Kilograms	

QUESTION 2

Using the following columns, place the words under the correct column. The first one has been done for you.

~~Kilograms~~   Litres   Metres   Grams   Centimetres   Pounds   Kilometres   Inches   Gallons   Stones   Millilitres   Millimetres   Tonnes

Metric Measurements	Imperial Measurements
Kilograms	

QUESTION 3

Which metric unit would be most suitable to measure in for the area of a school playing field?

A – Centimetres

B – Miles

C – Metres

D – Tonnes

Answer [　　　　　　　　　　　　]

QUESTION 4

Which imperial unit would be most suitable to measure the weight of a bag of potatoes?

A – Cubic Inches

B – Tonnes

C – Gallons

D – Pounds

Answer [　　　　　　　　　　　　]

QUESTION 5

Circle the measurement which is closest to the imperial measurement.

a) **10 miles**   16km   1000 m   16,000 cm

b) **12 inches**   30mm   30cm   3 m

c) **4 pints**   2 l   20 l   200 ml

QUESTION 6

James cycles 4,340 metres. Matthew cycles 4.04 kilometres.

Who cycled the furthest? Explain your answer using examples.

_____

_____

_____

_____

_____

QUESTION 7

Convert the following:

a) 5 hours and 20 minutes into minutes.

b) 730 minutes into hours and minutes.

c) 19 foot into inches.

d) 20,000cm³ in litres

e) 150 pounds in ounces.

Answers

Q1.

Length	Weight	Capacity/Volume
Metres Centimetres Kilometres Inches Millimetres	Kilograms Grams Pounds	Litres, Millilitres

Q2.

Metric Measurements	Imperial Measurements
Kilograms Litres Metres Grams Centimetres Kilometres Millilitres Millimetres	Pounds Inches Gallons Stones Tonnes

Q3.

C - Metres

Q4.

D - Pounds

METRIC AND IMPERIAL UNITS

Q5.

   a) 10 miles ≈ 16 km

   b) 12 inches ≈ 30 cm

   c) 4 pints ≈ 2 l

Q6.

James cycled the furthest.

- You need to begin by working in the same units of measurement.
- Let's change Matthew's distance into metres = 4.04 kilometres = 4040 metres.
- That means that James cycled the furthest.

Q7.

   a) 320 minutes

      - There are 60 minutes in 1 hour.
      - 60 x 5 = 300
      - 300 + 20 = 320 minutes

   b) 12 hours and 10 minutes

      - There are 60 minutes in 1 hour.
      - 730 ÷ 60 = 12.166…
      - So that means there are 12 whole hours (12 x 60 = 720)
      - 730 – 720 = 10 minutes
      - 12 hours and 10 minutes

c) 228 inches
- There are 12 inches in 1 foot.
- 19 x 12 = 228 inches

d) 20 litres
- There are 1000 cm³ in 1 litre.
- 20,000 ÷ 1,000 = 20 litres

e) 2,400 ounces
- There are 16 ounces in 1 pound.
- 16 x 150 = 2,400 ounces

HOW ARE YOU GETTING ON?

SPEED, DISTANCE AND TIME

SPEED, DISTANCE AND TIME

You need to know the relationship between speed, distance and time.

Sometimes, you will be required to work out one of the above, based on the information you are given. To do this, there is a simple formula that you **MUST** remember:

REMEMBER THIS FORMULA!

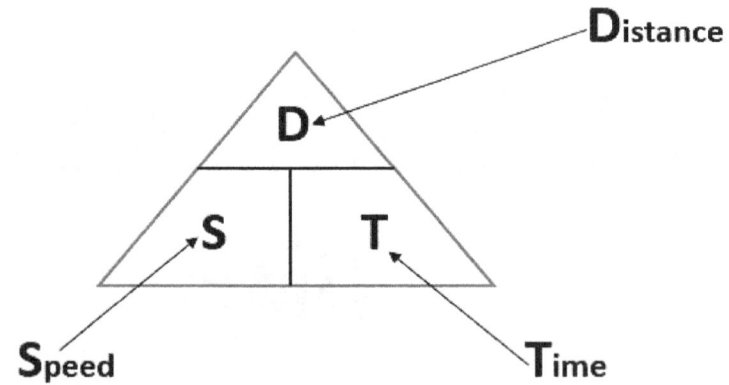

You can use the above formula to work out any question relating to speed, distance or time.

Of course, you need to know what to do with the formula. It's quite easy actually, all you have to do is cover up the letter that you are trying to work out, and then do the calculation that is left.

On the next page, I have provided examples of how to work out each variable.

SPEED, DISTANCE AND TIME

HOW TO WORK OUT SPEED

To work out the average speed, place your thumb over the speed variable ('S'), and then do the calculation.

EXAMPLE

What speed covers 34 miles in 10 minutes?

Step 1

As we are working out speed, we will have to divide the distance by the time.

Step 2

How many times does 10 (minutes) go into 60? (1 hour) = 6

Step 3

Speed = 34 x 6 = 204 mph

HOW TO WORK OUT DISTANCE

To work out the distance travelled, place your thumb over the distance variable ('D'), and then work out the equation.

DISTANCE
(SPEED x TIME)

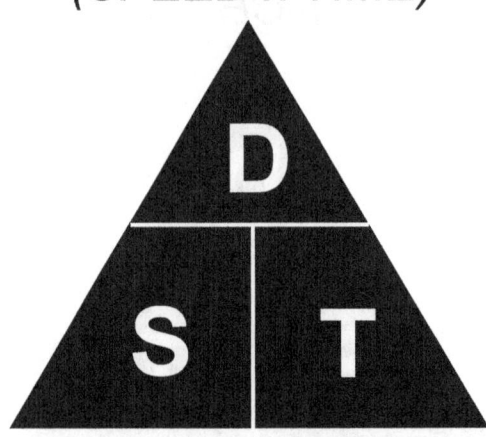

EXAMPLE

How far do you travel in 1 hour and 30 minutes at a constant speed of 40 mph?

Step 1

We know that, to work out the distance, we must multiply the speed by the time.

Step 2

40 x 1.5 (1 hour and 30 minutes is 1.5) = 60 miles

HOW TO WORK OUT TIME

To work out the time taken, place your thumb over the time variable ('T'), and then work out the equation.

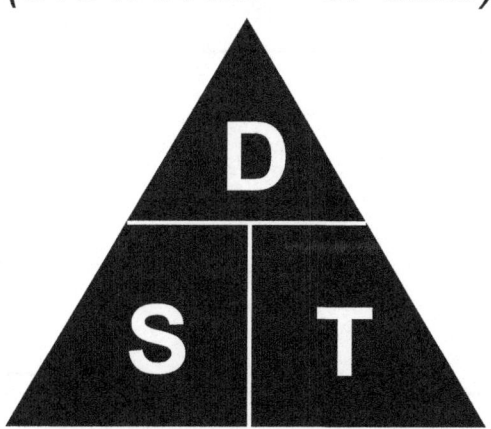

EXAMPLE

How long does it take to travel 48 miles at 20 mph?

Step 1

We know that the formula for calculating time = distance ÷ speed
Time = 48/20

Step 2

Following the same method used to calculate speed, the denominator needs to go into 60 (minutes).

In this case, 20 will go into 60 three times:

Time = 48/20

Time = 48 x 3 (3 x 20 = 60 minutes)

Step 3

Time = 144 minutes (2 hours and 24 minutes)

Question Time!

QUESTION 1

Marty runs 20 kilometres in 2 hours. What is his average speed in km/h?

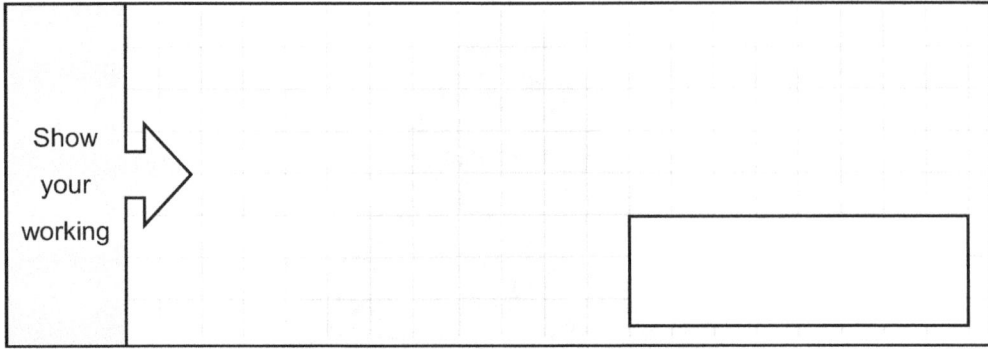

QUESTION 2

A car travelled 100 metres in 9.63 seconds. On a second occasion, it travelled 200 metres in 19.32 seconds. Which distance had the greater average speed?

A	B	C	D
100 metres	200 metres	Both the same	Cannot say

QUESTION 3

Lisa cycles at an average speed of 8km/h. How far does she travel if she cycles for 4 hours?

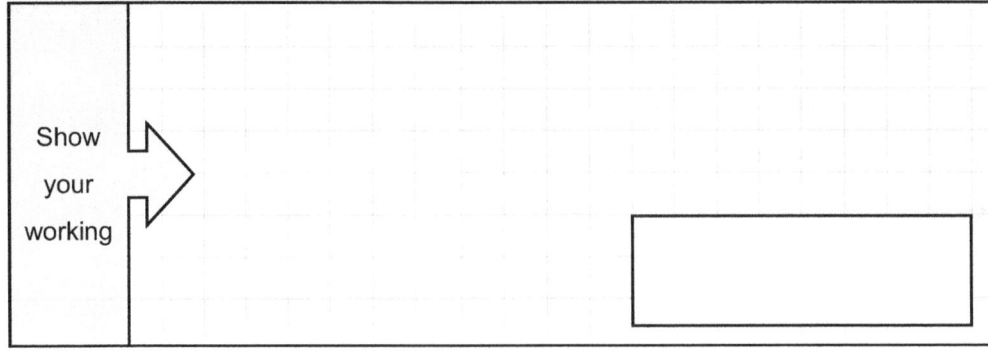

SPEED, DISTANCE AND TIME

QUESTION 4

James runs from 4.50pm until 5.20pm at an average speed of 7 km/h. How far did he go?

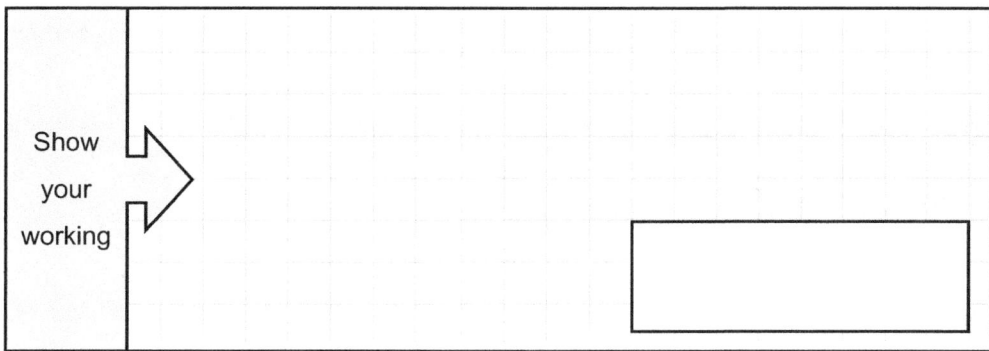

QUESTION 5

A lorry travels at a speed of 60 mph for 90 miles. How long will the journey take?

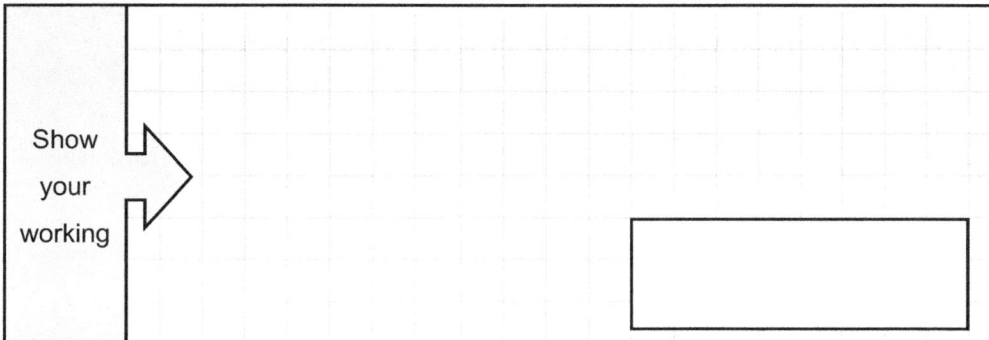

QUESTION 6

A skier travels 1,000 metres in 100 seconds. What was the average speed of the skier?

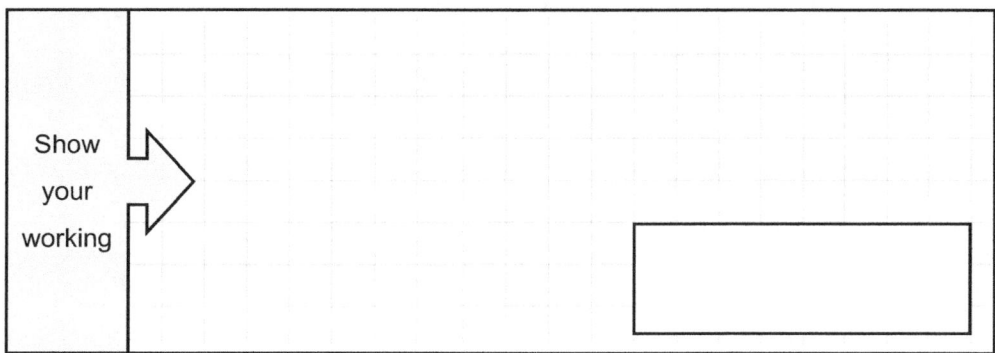

Answers

Q1.

10 km/h

- 20 ÷ 2 = 10 km/h

Q2.

A = 100 metres

- 100 ÷ 9.63 = 10.384.
- 200 ÷ 19.32 = 10.351.
- Therefore 100 metres has the greatest average speed.

Q3.

32 km

- So, 8 x 4 = 32 km

Q4.

3.5 km

- 4.50 pm – 5.20pm = 30 minutes.
- 30 minutes = 0.5 hour.
- So, distance = 7 x 0.5 = 3.5 km.

SPEED, DISTANCE AND TIME

Q5.

1 hour and 30 minutes

- 90 miles divided by 60 = 1.5 hours.

Q6.

10 m/s

- 1,000 ÷ 100 = 10 m/s

HOW ARE YOU GETTING ON?

DENSITY, MASS AND VOLUME

DENSITY, MASS AND VOLUME

You need to know the relationship between density, mass and volume.

Sometimes, you will be required to work out one of the above, based on the information you are given. To do this, there is a simple formula that you **MUST** remember:

REMEMBER THIS FORMULA!

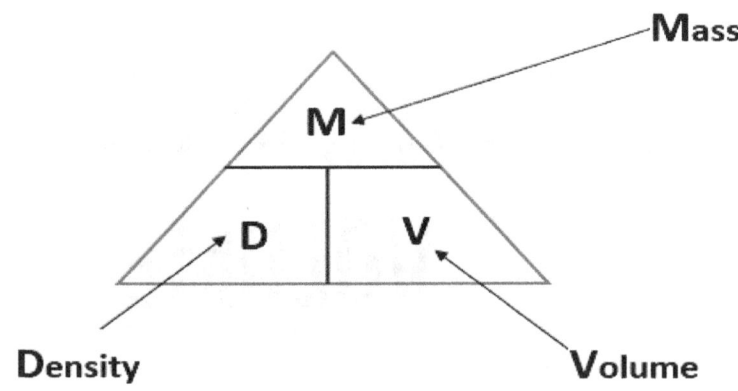

You can use the above formula to work out any question relating to mass, density and volume.

Of course, you need to know what to do with the formula. Luckily, it's quite easy! All you have to do is cover up the letter that you are trying to work out, and then do the calculation that is left.

On the next page, I have provided examples of how to work out each variable.

DENSITY, MASS AND VOLUME

HOW TO WORK OUT MASS

To work out the mass, place your thumb over the mass variable ('M'), and then do the calculation.

MASS
(DENSITY x VOLUME)

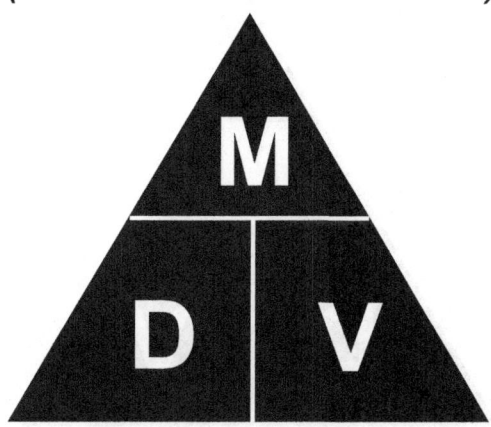

EXAMPLE

A gold watch has a density of 16.5 g/cm³. It has a volume of 100 cm³.

Work out the mass (in grams) of the gold watch.

Step 1

The formula to work out mass is density x volume.

Step 2

16.5 x 100 = 1,650 g

HOW TO WORK OUT DENSITY

To work out the density, place your thumb over the density variable ('D'), and then do the calculation.

DENSITY
(MASS ÷ VOLUME)

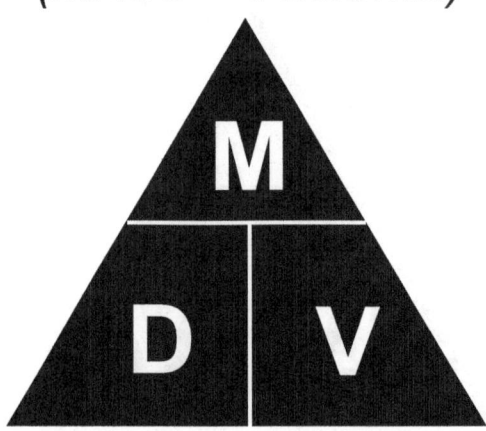

EXAMPLE

A pie weighs 200 grams and has a volume of 250 cm³.

Work out the density of the pie.

Step 1

To work out the density, you must use the formula: mass ÷ volume.

Step 2

200 ÷ 250 = 0.8 g/cm³

DENSITY, MASS AND VOLUME 143

HOW TO WORK OUT VOLUME

To work out the volume, place your thumb over the volume variable ('V'), and then do the calculation.

VOLUME
(MASS ÷ DENSITY)

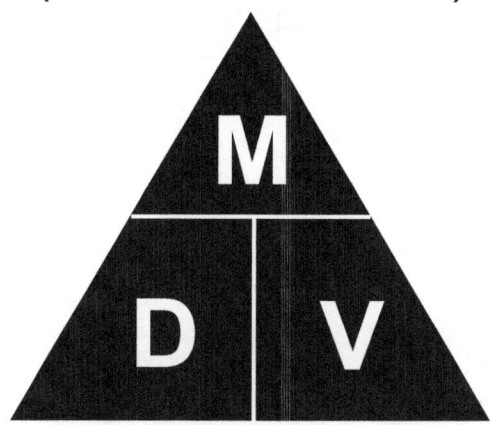

EXAMPLE

A pile of metal weighs 2,000 grams, with a density of 40 g/cm³.

What is the volume of the pile of metal?

Step 1

To work out the volume, you should use the formula: mass ÷ density.

Step 2

2,000 ÷ 40 = 50cm³

Question Time!

QUESTION 1

An object weighs 10,000 grams, with a density of 125 g/cm³.

Work out the volume of the object.

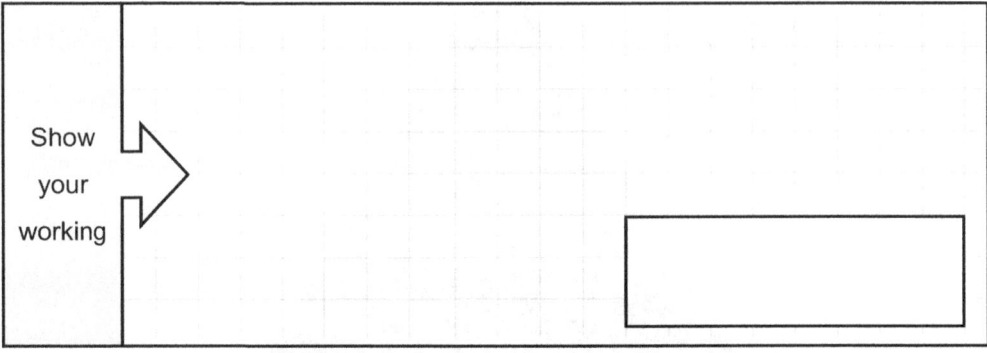

QUESTION 2

An item of jewellery has a density of 6.7 g/cm³, with a volume of 15 cm³.

Work out the mass of the item of jewellery. Write your answer in grams (g).

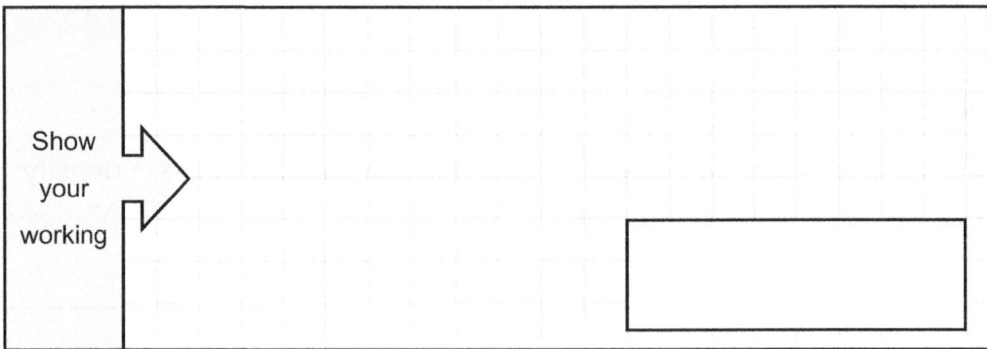

QUESTION 3

An object weighs 1,500 grams and has a volume of 2,000 cm³.

Work out the density of the object.

Show your working

QUESTION 4

Complete the wordsearch below.

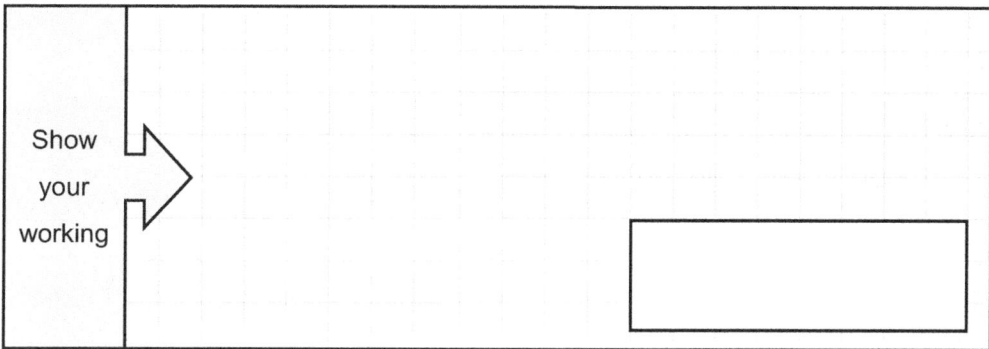

MASS
VOLUME
DENSITY
UNIT
GRAMS
CENTIMETRES
VALUE
FORMULA
KILOGRAMS
WEIGHT
CUBED

Answers

Q1.

80 cm³

- 10,000 ÷ 125 = 80 cm³

Q2.

100.5 grams

- 6.7 x 15 = 100.5 grams

Q3.

0.75 g/cm³

- 1,500 ÷ 2,000 = 0.75 g/cm³

Q4.

```
O R Y I C U N D S A A O X M Z T D E B Z
M Q F H H A G Q A P F D Z D B F R B M F
H T I W Z G N M Y W B M Y Y V B O N C Y
E U Q R I T I T T F S J N G A K W C K O
E P Q U S A S Y I C Y H V J V J E O G S
T W D A A G S Z S N T N L Y O W E T M E
W W N E T K A K N I U A C E T B I A M C
F Y W N T Z M D E B O D N N V B R U O R
I S K T Z D O W D K U L Z C F G L A L F
L X D I U S B S Y J Q T Q B X O U Z I Q
Q F X M D B R T S L W E T Q V T I O P N
M G W E C A L U M R O F L S F T F Z E G
O F Q T P C O E L E G J U M J H R P X I
D C M R D F E G X X B L M A Y G K W I I
J U S E A Y Q S L G Y V U R C I C J P O
A O B S O M P T G H O Y Y G D E U B E B
F U R X Q M B O O T G B I O W W U M E D
C M L M J B P K A R H L T L N A O L O L
Y A A A T D H Z Y I F E V I S C J N A N
B E E M C H L E J B V Y T K S Z U Z J V
```

HOW ARE YOU GETTING ON?

MAPS AND SCALING

USING MAP SCALES

Map scales can be used to show the distance on a map, in order to represent the actual distance in real life.

1 cm = 5 km

'1 cm represents 5 kilometres'

⊢――⊥――⊣ 0 1 2	1 cm = 5 km 2 cm = 10 km	1 cm represents 5 km So, 2 cm would represent 10 km

HOW TO CONVERT BETWEEN MAP SCALES AND REAL LIFE

It is important that you are comfortable with converting map scales into real life sizes, and vice versa.

Key things to remember:

Your scale will always be in the form of = 1 cm = ...

To find the real-life distance, you would need to **MULTIPLY** the scale.

To find the map scale, you would need to **DIVIDE** by the scale.

ALWAYS CHECK TO SEE WHETHER YOUR ANSWER LOOKS RIGHT!

MAPS AND SCALING | 151

EXAMPLE 1

Destination A and Destination B are located near one another. Using the scale of 1 cm = 5 km, work out how far, in kilometres, the places are apart if it was drawn 8 cm away on a map.

Step 1

You've been given the scale of 1 cm = 5 km.

Step 2

Because you are trying to work out the real-life distance, you will need to **MULTIPLY** by the scale:

- 5 x 8 = 40 kilometres.

Have a go at drawing a map scale with the above information!
Remember to use a ruler!

EXAMPLE 2

Destination A and Destination B are located near one another. Using the scale of 1 cm = 6 km, work out how part the destinations will be drawn apart, if their distance was 72 kilometres.

Step 1

You've been given the scale of 1 cm = 6 km.

Step 2

Because you are trying to work out the map scale, you will need to **DIVIDE** by the scale:

- 72 ÷ 6 = 12 cm

Have a go at drawing a map scale with the above information!
Remember to use a ruler!

SCALE DRAWINGS

Scale drawings are very similar to maps. The same rules apply as mentioned on the previous pages, so it's important that you know them!

Instead of a map, a scale drawing will often be drawn onto grid paper.

You will still be given the rule of '1 cm = …'

You will either be asked to work out the lengths and widths of the drawing, **OR**, you will be able to draw the diagram yourself based on the information given to you.

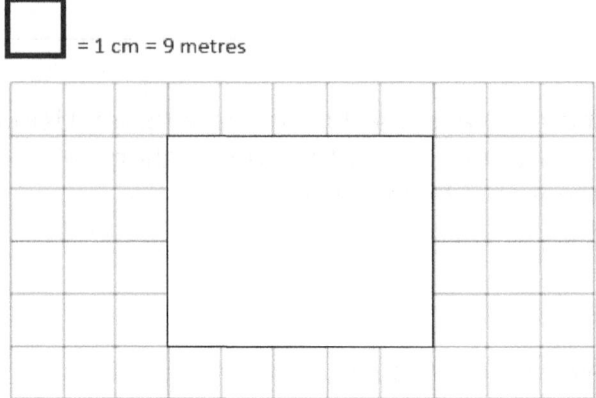

☐ = 1 cm = 9 metres

1cm = 9 metres

- That means the length of the rectangle is = 9 x 5 = 45 metres

- The width of the rectangle is = 9 x 4 = 36 metres

Sometimes, you may be required to use compass directions. This is exactly the same process as you've learnt.

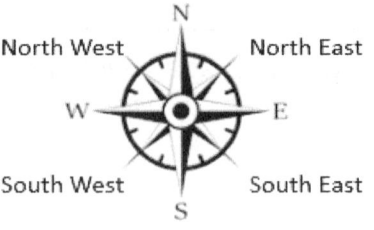

MAPS AND SCALING 153

Question Time!

QUESTION 1

Here is a map of an island.

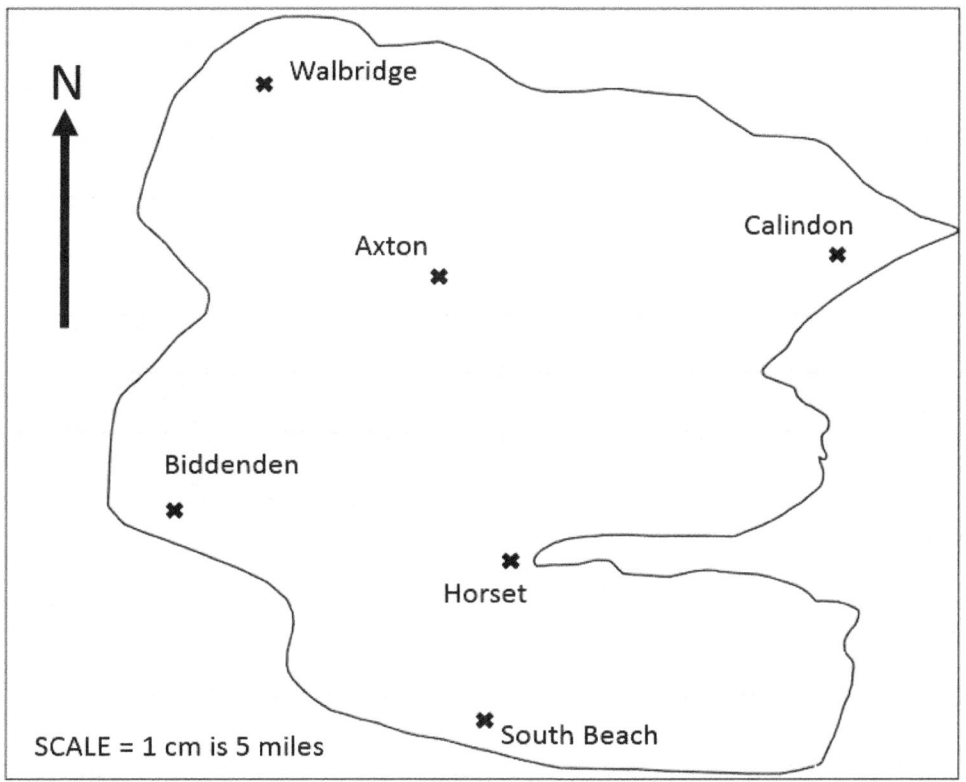

a) Using the map scale, work out the distance between Walbridge and Axton.

_____
_____
_____
_____

b) Using the map scale, work out the distance been South Beach and Horset.

___

c) Using the map scale, work out the distance between Biddenden and Calindon.

___

QUESTION 2

A scale of a map is 1 cm : 30,000 km. A distance is measured as 4 cm on a map.

How many kilometres is this equivalent based on the scale of the map?

KILOMETRES ___

QUESTION 3

For the following statements, write your answers:

The scale of a map is 1 cm = 13 metres. How many centimetres would the map scale be if the distance was 117 metres?

MAPS AND SCALING

We are trying to work out the distance between Country A and Country B. If a map scale was 1 cm = 6 miles, how many miles is it if the map scale was 14 cm?

[ ]

QUESTION 4

Below is a map showing different storage lock ups.

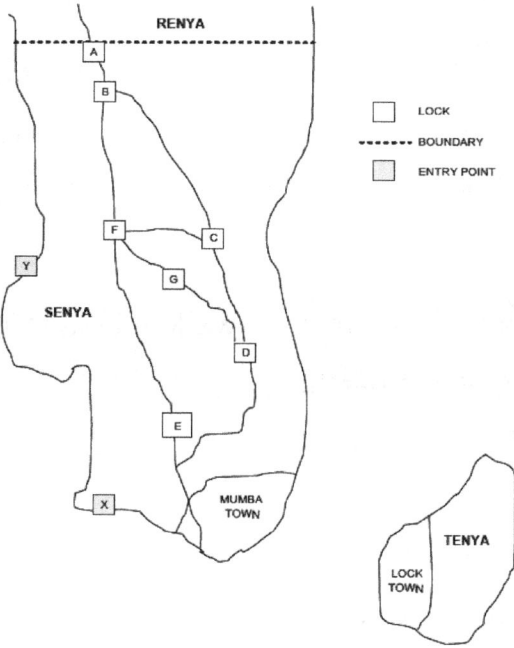

If the scale of the map is 1 cm = 19 km, work out the distance, using a straight line, between lock-up A and lock-up X.

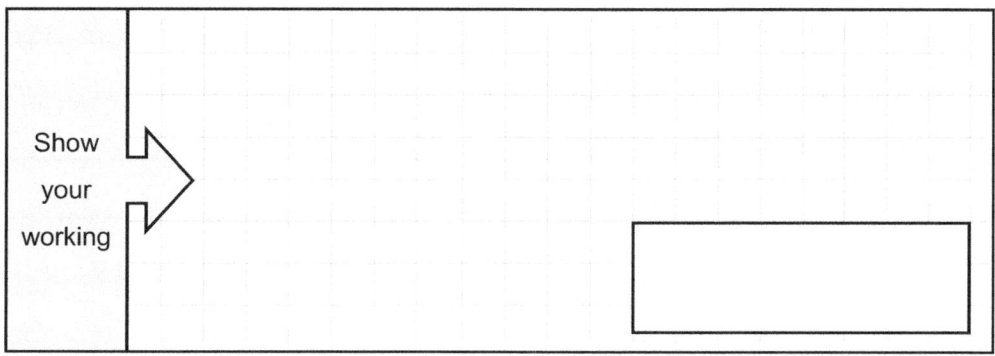

Show your working

QUESTION 5

This is a scale drawing of Derick's back and front garden.

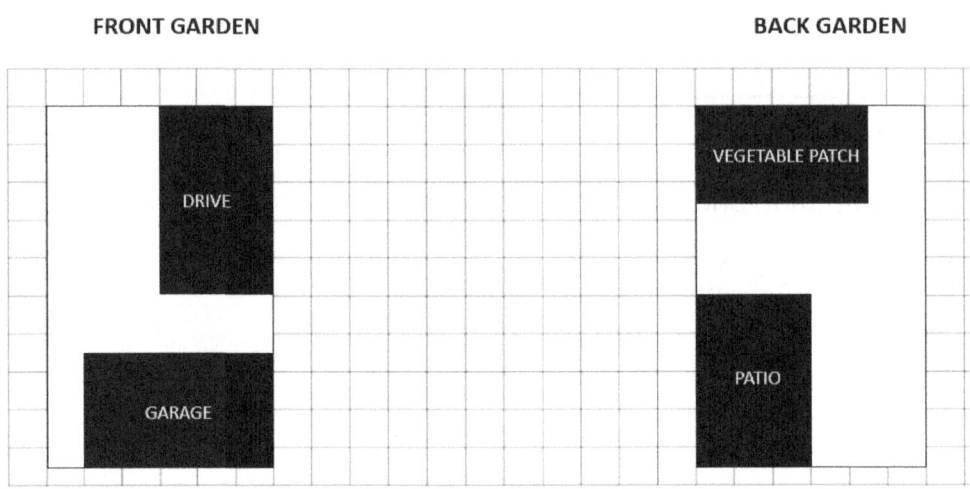

If the map scale is 1 cm = 2 metres, work out the following:

a) Length of vegetable patch: _____

   Width of vegetable patch: _____

b) Length of garage: _____

   Width of garage: _____

c) Length of drive: _____

   Width of drive: _____

d) Length of patio: _____

   Width of patio: _____

MAPS AND SCALING

Answers

Q1.

a) 17.5 miles
- 3.5cm x 5 = 17.5 miles

b) 10 miles
- 2cm x 5 = 10 miles

c) 47.5 miles
- 9.5cm x 5 = 47.5 miles

Q2.

120,000 kilometres
- 4 x 30,000 = 120,000 km

Q3.

a) 9 cm
- 117 ÷ 13 = 9cm

b) 84 miles
- 14 x 6 = 84 miles

Q4.

114 kilometres
- 6 x 19 km = 114 kilometres

Q5.

a) Length of vegetable patch: (4.5 x 2) = 9 metres
Width of vegetable patch: (2.5 x 2) = 5 metres

b) Length of garage: (5 x 2) = 10 metres
Width of garage: (3 x 2) = 6 metres

c) Length of drive: (3 x 2) = 6 metres
Width of drive: (5 x 2) = 10 metres

d) Length of patio: (3 x 2) = 6 metres
Width of patio: (4.5 x 2) = 9 metres

HOW ARE YOU GETTING ON?

NEED A LITTLE EXTRA HELP WITH KEY STAGE THREE (KS3) MATHS?

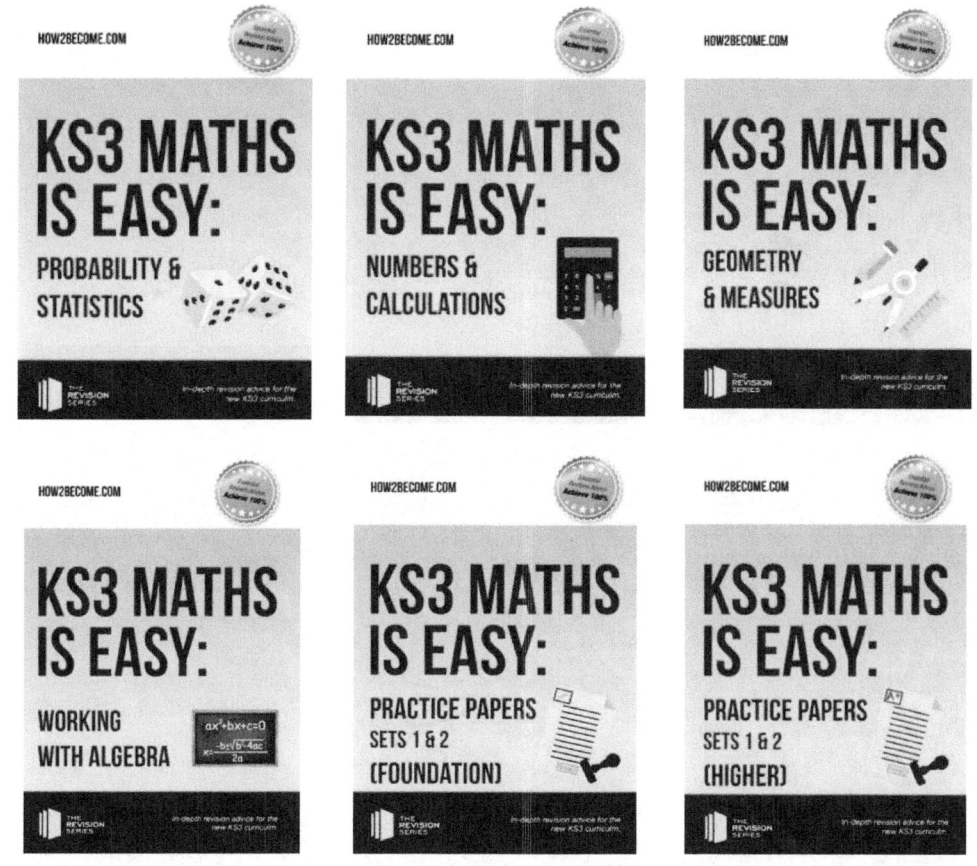

How2Become have created these other FANTASTIC guides to help you and your child prepare for their Key Stage Three (KS3) Maths assessments.

FOR MORE INFORMATION ON OUR KEY STAGE 3 (KS3) MATHS GUIDES, PLEASE CHECK OUT THE FOLLOWING:

WWW.HOW2BECOME.COM

WANT TO TAKE A LOOK AT OUR KEY STAGE THREE (KS3) ENGLISH GUIDES?

How2Become have created these other FANTASTIC guides to help you and your child prepare for their Key Stage Three (KS3) English assessments.

FOR MORE INFORMATION ON OUR KEY STAGE 3 (KS3) ENGLISH GUIDES, PLEASE CHECK OUT THE FOLLOWING:

WWW.HOW2BECOME.COM

  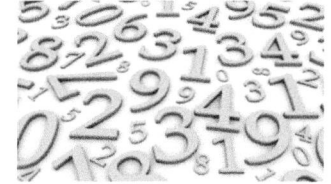

Get Access To

FREE

Key Stage 3 Resources

www.MyEducationalTests.co.uk

Printed and bound by CPI Group (UK) Ltd, Croydon, CR0 4YY
03/02/2026
02046931-0001